Dear Nana:
Grandmother Tales of Love, Secrets and Going Home

edited by

Robyn M. McGee

PEGASUS BOOKS

Pegasus Books
3338 San Marino Ave
San Jose, CA 95127
www.pegasusbooks.net

First Edition: May 2015

Published in North America by Pegasus Books. For information, please contact Pegasus Books c/o Christopher Moebs, 3338 San Marino Ave, San Jose, CA 95127.

Library of Congress Cataloguing-In-Publication Data
Robyn McGee
Dear Nana: Grandmother Tales of Love, Secrets, and Going Home/Robyn McGee – [1st] ed
p. cm.
Library of Congress Control Number: 2015938937
ISBN – 978-1-941859-27-8
1. BODY, MIND & SPIRIT / Inspiration & Personal Growth. 2. FAMILY & RELATIONSHIPS / Parenting / Grandparenting. 3. LITERARY COLLECTIONS / Essays 4. BIOGRAPHY & AUTOBIOGRAPHY / Personal Memoirs 5. FAMILY & RELATIONSHIPS / General. 6. HISTORY / General.

10   9   8   7   6   5   4   3   2   1

Comments about *Dear Nana* and requests for additional copies, book club rates and author speaking appearances may be addressed to Robyn McGee or Pegasus Books c/o Christopher Moebs, 3338 San Marino Ave, San Jose, CA, 95127, or you can send your comments and requests via e-mail to cmoebs@pegasusbooks.net.

Also available as an eBook from Internet retailers and from Pegasus Books

Printed in the United States of America

To Jeanne.
You left before you could read Dear Nana
but your last words as always
were filled with
love and encouragement. RIP.

My grandmother, she started walking five miles a day when she was 60. She's 97 today and we don't know where the hell she is.
Ellen DeGeneres

Dear Nana: Grandmother Tales of Love, Secrets and Going Home is a collection of 40 unusual, true life stories from writers around the world about an incomparable relationship.

TO MARCELLE —

MY WONDERFUL COACH

AND EVEN BETTER FRIEND.

MANY THANKS FOR HELPING

ME FIND MY VOICE.

Alice Walker

Dear Nana: Grandmother Tales of Love, Secrets and Going Home

TABLE OF CONTENTS

TABLE OF CONTENTS cont.

TABLE OF CONTENTS cont.

TABLE OF CONTENTS cont.

Preface

Recalling lessons from their Grandmothers for inspiration, writers young and old from around the world share stories of bonds between elders and children so tight her smile, silent disappointments, secrets kept and the smells of her kitchen are remembered and cherished many years later. A few of the *Dear Nana* writers yearn for a woman they will never know; a surprising number report actually seeing and speaking to their grandmothers after her death.

The Nana Tales is an uncommon collection with universal themes of love and loss, joy and pain, dreams lost and dreams come true and the enduring power of family.

The multicultural contributors include a 10-year-old Indian protege from Washington DC (A Dream Come True), a mother of four who lives with her wife on a farm in Connecticut (Don't Tell Joe), the wife of an Oscar winning composer (The True Story of my Great Gram), a feminist clinical researcher from the Caribbean (Gracie), an American student living in Croatia (She Floats Inside My Head), a Midwestern woman whose grandmother was the first American to give birth to her own grandchildren (Surrogate Grandmother), a British marine biologist (Granny takes the Burnt Toast) and dozens of other voices who pay tribute to their grandmothers with reverence and realism.

The *Dear Nana* tales demonstrate how a grandmother's love can take many forms. It's about sharing snacks in a darkened theater (Movies with Nana), baking indescribably scrumptious dinners and desserts (Grandma's Special Ingredient, Grandma's Kitchen) and traveling many miles to retrieve a lost toy (Departures). The grandmothers here are complex and imperfect women who often put their grandkids' interests before the children they birthed. She embodies infinite patience and understanding, though not always; a few writers recall grandmothers who were critical and distant (Loose Seams) or existing only through the memories of the generations who knew her (The Girl in the Gold Dress).

Gathering the *Dear Nana* tales, I was particularly astonished by the number of writers who describe how their grandmothers came back to visit them one last time after their death (Epistle for Nana, Lighting Up with Alice, Grandma Martha). Skeptics will say the visions were merely childlike attempts to hold on to the woman they deeply loved. Others will believe it's proof of the otherworldly sway of grandmothers.

Reading the *Dear Nana* tales, sometimes into the wee hours of the morning, I felt honored to get to know even a small part of these families and their grandmothers, some still living, others deceased. The privilege of reading the memories and telling their stories left me with a profound sense of longing and loss. It had never occurred to me before that I, like many people, had a grandmother who was "known and unknown." I can count on one hand the occasions I spent time with either of my grandmothers. My father's mother who we called Mo Mo was gentle and strong and when she hugged me I wanted to live in her bosom forever. My other grandmother, Estelle, I met only once and know her mainly through family secrets uncovered. It reminds me of what anthropologist Margaret Mead once said, "Everyone needs to have access both to grandparents and grandchildren in order to be a full human being."

Lastly, having spent close to two years with the *Dear Nana* tales, I now feel somewhat like a parent sending her child off to school to the care of others. Hopefully, *Dear Nana* will inspire you to recall all the love and contradictions you may have had with your own grandmother and to appreciate her even more.

If you are interested in sharing a story about your grandmother, write me at **staycalm09@gmail.com**.

Robyn McGee
Editor

Epistle for Nan
By William Poe

Dear Nan,

I can't believe a decade has passed. As the old adage goes, "it seems like yesterday, but it was long ago." Well, no matter how much time passes, life has gotten only a little easier without you. Your beautiful face remains frozen in time in my mind.

I wanted to sit down and pen these thoughts to you and wasn't sure where to start. It's impossible to encapsulate forty years of precious time together in any one letter and would not do our time together justice to attempt to do so. From the time I was born and through the next four decades, you would be a principal navigator in my life, often helping to steer me back on course when I ran adrift.

It wasn't the forsythia branch that you had us break off the front yard tree that kept us in line as you may have thought, but our respect and love for you. The switching from the branch never hurt us nearly as much. Knowing we had shown even the slightest irreverence towards you hurt your grandsons more.

Now, at fifty years old, I sure could use some navigation from you, as life's choices do not seem to get any easier. I keep that cardboard kaleidoscope you bought for me when I was five on a shelf in my office. And whenever I want to be transported back to your house on Arcadia Avenue, where I spent much of my time growing up, I give the kaleidoscope a turn or two. Each dazzling swirl of those antique glass beads transports me back to my fantastical childhood. I smile at the memory of the teaspoon of sugar and whiskey you would sometimes give us before bed when we were ailing to help lull us to sleep. Is this where my fondness for libations derived?

At breakfast you would cut my toast into perfect tiny squares and along with a piece of egg white, dip them into the

yolk and sing 'eensy teensy spider' so that I would eat, all the
while moving our fingers up the spout and down the drain.
You would gently put mercurochrome on my many cuts and
scrapes, and lightly blow on the medicine to accelerate the
healing.

Nor will I ever forget those hot and muggy summer eves
as we patiently awaited those tiny sporadic lights to flicker in
your yard. With jar in hand we would attempt to snatch a
hovering firefly from its flight to secure it, and with deft
precision you would remove its light while still glowing and
make rings to put on our fingers. During late nights, the faint
glow of a black and white television would slip beneath the
cracks of a door and into my bedroom as you sat and
watched Perry Mason into the wee hours of the morning, and
your slight crunching of ice or cracking of chewing gum
would interrupt the night's tranquility. I will never forget
those long journeys we made to Florida, watching the
mermaids at Weeki Wachee Springs. And how before you
quit smoking, you would summon me over to the table as you
played cards with your sisters and give me a bedtime kiss,
leaving the same deep red lipstick trace on my cheek that lay
on your cigarette.

You taught me to kneel before my bedside each night
and say prayers before tucking me in. Some of my most
cherished possessions from you are your handwritten letters,
the ones you wrote so faithfully each week while I was in the
Marine Corps. Your endearing, encouraging words comforted
your grandson on many lonely nights thousands of miles
away. I have each letter you ever wrote, yet cannot bring
myself to reread them since your passing.

You loved making Sunday dinners, searching for four
leaf clovers, playing rummy, and gardening. Hydrangeas were
your favorite. But most of all, you devoted your life to taking
care of your grandchildren. And although you bore no
children of your own, you raised us as yours. You never
realized we knew you had adopted mom; it would have

pained you if you did. However, it only made you more special and endearing to all of us.

November fifth is surely a day I do not wish to relive, yet it is a day I will never forget. It was the day you transitioned from the earthly world to who knows where. It was the darkest day of my life.

The day before, we sat together in your hospital room listening to our favorite singer, Nat King Cole.

"Oh, that man can sing," I remember you saying.

We held hands and talked. I told you how you were the best grandmother anyone could ever have. You asked how my sisters were doing and told me to be sure to tell them how much you loved them. They didn't visit because they were young and scared to see you in this condition. We watched Wheel of Fortune as we always did, and I kissed you goodnight and said I would see you the next day. The following morning, we got word that you were improving and thinking that you were out of the woods, I didn't visit as planned. Instead, I drank in celebration that night, toasting your homecoming, which would surely be forthcoming. An ominous storm rose from out of nowhere that evening, foreshadowing what would become of the following day.

There you lay in your hospital bed, just as I had left you two days earlier. You looked so peaceful. I held your beautifully crooked fingers in my hands, and then kissed your lips, weeping uncontrollably. Your soul had taken flight. The nurse was puzzled when I asked for a pair of scissors. I snipped a lock of your hair and placed it in a piece of tissue and handed it to mom.

We held your wake in our home just like they did in the old days. Your silky silvery hair lay across the cotton pillow and flowed like a weeping willow. Dressed in your favorite pink blouse, you were as beautiful in death as in life.

I sat with you late into the wee hours of the morning, listening to the haunting voice of Eva Cassidy singing "Fields of Gold." It would be one of our last moments we shared. The night before, I drove to the cemetery and lay inside your empty, freshly dug grave and gazed up into the chilly November skies. A shooting star whisked by. Was it you Nan?

For endless days, weeks, months, I was tethered to a bed, attempting to embalm my body with any ingredients that would take away the pain. Pills and alcohol brought only temporary relief. You came to me in my dreams and that helped pull me through that awful time.

"Penny for your thoughts," you would always ask as my head lay in your lap, your fingers massaging my temples. I would give ten years of my life to have you back for just one more day to hear your sweet voice again.

To steal a line from our favorite Nat King Cole song, "I miss you most of all my darling, when autumn leaves start to fall."

Until we meet again.

Your loving grandson,

Billy

Battlescars
By Chynna Laird

My grandmother Lillian was a stubborn, feisty woman who was as fiercely protective of her family as a mother bear is with her cubs. I believe these characteristics fueled her strength to fight and survive breast cancer—twice. Even more remarkable, Grandma contracted the disease during the 1950s. Oddly our family never talked about my grandmother's illness but even as a child I knew something about Grandma was different.

I remember the times when Grandma got dressed up, she had a womanly figure. But when she was at home in her casual clothes, her shirts would hang flat. Maybe I wasn't supposed to notice. Maybe I wasn't supposed to ask questions. But one day Grandma and I found ourselves in an awkward position where we had to talk about it.

It was the summer I turned thirteen. I loved staying with my grandparents in their beautiful house in Winnipeg, but it was a distressing time in my young life. All my friends started showing the beginning signs of womanhood while I still looked like a boy with long hair.

"It'll happen soon enough," Grandma told me. "Don't be in such a rush to grow up, Dumplin. Besides, breasts are just an accessory. Being a woman goes far deeper than what is on the outside. Someday, I'll tell you about it."

That day came sooner than both of us expected. I rushed into her bedroom one morning to grab Grandpa's house keys and surprised Grandma while she was getting dressed.

"Oh… no… I'm so sorry…" I started to say. I wasn't ready for what I saw. Grandma stood there, her house dress open to her waist. Her fingertips held the zipper—frozen in their position. For the first time in my life, I understood why everyone always made sure Grandma's door was shut while she dressed.

"It's alright, child," Grandma said softly. "I left the door open. Didn't think anyone was still in the house. Please…come in."

I couldn't move. I felt deeply embarrassed, for her and for me. Grandma removed her hand from her zipper and brought it to her side. My eyes fixed on her chest. In the space where her breasts were supposed to have been were two large dents. The skin was discolored and there were purple lines that extended out, like those on a map. Some of them were swollen. Some lay flat and disappeared under her house dress towards her armpits. I'd always known something awful had happened to my Grandmother. I'd always wanted to ask but could never find the nerve.

My eyes flooded with tears, searching for the right words.

"Oh, Dumplin," Grandma said. "Don't be frightened. Grandma is just fine. I'm glad you came in. Grandpa always shuts the door because he doesn't want to have to talk about it. He's still scared, I guess."

I finally found my voice. "What… what happened?"

Grandma zipped up her house dress and motioned me to sit with her on the bed. "Many years ago, I got sick," Grandma began. "Very sick." She paused. "When they couldn't figure out why I wasn't able to shake what I thought was the flu, they ran some tests and found some lumps in my left breast. Well, after a lot of other tests, they found out it was cancer. Back in those days, they just removed the breast then gave you lots of medicine."

She continued calmly. "But they didn't get it all and Grandma had to go back. They took the right breast and some of the tissue under my arms called lymph nodes."

Lymph nodes? I squeezed hands in my armpits and hugged myself tight.

"Oh, now, don't you go worrying about things," she said. Grandma began stroking my hair. "It happened a long time ago. I'm not ashamed of it."

"Will it come back, Grandma? Will you get sick again?" I kept my hands in my armpits.

Grandma tilted her head at me like she always did when I asked something she needed to think about before she could answer me.

"I don't know. I hope not. But I can't worry about it. These things happen, you know?"

"Is that why you told me 'breasts are just an accessory'?"

Grandma laughed. "Yes, that's right. Breasts may make you look like a woman but I don't feel any less of a woman than I did with them. Maybe I'm even more so, because I didn't truly understand what it was to be one until my breasts were taken away. Doesn't change who you are, child. Just your form. Women are strong. We're fighters and still the head of the family, even without our breasts."

She winked at me, pointed to her chest and continued, "These are my battle scars, Dumplin. They are there to remind me I won the battle and I'll win the war."

I hugged Grandma hard. It didn't seem to matter anymore when I finally developed breasts. After our talk, my grandparents' bedroom door wasn't shut tight anymore, unless Grandpa was getting dressed. Even though she's been gone for over twenty years now, Grandma's words still sing in my ears whenever I put my hand over the little pink ribbon I proudly wear on my shirt (over my size AA breasts). Being a woman does go far deeper than what is on the outside.

And, someday, we'll win this war.

Gracie
By Cherise Charleswell

It is a behavior I came to know as normal. It was an arrangement formed long before I was born and long before my mother and my aunts were conceived. To call my Grandmother Gracie the "other woman" greatly diminishes her role; she was BoBo's "co-wife" for over 40 years.

By the time that I was a preteen, I knew my beloved Gracie led the kind of life I could never live. I am not stating my preference and desire to be in a completely monogamous relationship as a means to bash my grandmother. I realize that our family is complex, but certainly not far from the norm in the Virgin Islands, and within the greater Caribbean in general. Hell, truth be told, most of the people who reside in the Virgin Islands can trace their heritage—be it a parent, grandparent, great parent—to a neighboring island. In my grandmother Gracie's case, that heritage would be Puerto Rico, and the smallest of the Virgin Islands, St John, a place with a rich history and notoriously proud people.

He would visit often, the man who was my Grandfather. We called him BoBo. Typically, Gracie welcomed BoBo with a smile so bright it could light one thousand candles. Of course Gracie always followed the unwritten rule in our family which limits physical contact, even a brief embrace.

I remember sitting and watching my grandmother Gracie and my grandfather on the front porch, where the two of them basked in the sunshine, sipping bittersweet beverages, such as a Malta India or a tall glass of maubi. It was on the front porch where the two of them would go to "pound melee"- hold counsel and discuss the topics of the day. I would try discreetly to stretch my ears to listen about what Miss So-and-So was doing, who had a new child or grandchild, and of course a favorite topic among Caribbean people, who was going to or coming from the States.

When my cousins and I made our way outside of the house, dashing across the constantly congested road, past the glass beer bottles en route to the playground, the two of them would watch us run by. Granny always had her chair perched in prime viewing position, ensuring that she would be able to see exactly who was coming and going, whether by foot or by car. The passersby would often stop to wave from their vehicles, or walk right over to hail up Miss Gracie. Others, who were unknown to my grandmother, would too offer the customary "Good Mawning" (afternoon or night). Often times, those who stopped by or shouted out greetings, readily became the next topic of conversation between Gracie and BoBo.

Though complicated, my extended family never seemed odd to me, and is actually quite common in Caribbean families. Even my father was born to a married man and a young single woman, who was already a mother of two. I think of these arrangements and how common they are in the Caribbean, so much so that those involved are not stigmatized or treated like social outcasts, like unwed mothers in the States had traditionally been. Nor are the delicate and intricate details of the relationships discussed openly in public or among family members. In short, our attitude is "It is what it is."

Furthermore, despite these overlapping ties, we are all raised to be aware of and to be able to quickly respond to the common inquiry of "who yuh for?" meaning who is your family, parents, and grandparents. Knowing these links intimately has helped me avoid awkward moments by being able to identify cousins and other blood relatives upon meeting for the first time; particularly those who mistakenly attempt to "rap" (flirt) to me not realizing we are related.

My uncle Gavin, another one of BoBo's children who was not conceived by his wife, shared with me what it was like when he first was taken to meet Gracie. He noted that she was warm, smiling, and cracking jokes with BoBo. Gracie had no harsh words for Gavin. She fed him, and nonchalantly gestured towards her own children, my mother and aunts and said, "dese here are BoBo's children dem."

Gavin recalls how funny and entertaining it was to be around Gracie, with her ready smile and lack of a filter. (A trait I have proudly inherited. Like Gracie, I find myself surrounded by folks who are laughing hysterically, and me wondering, what did I say?) Gavin admired Gracie's capacity for kindness and for always retaining a calm demeanor.

I now understand how Gracie's stoicism lead to much confusion for me and even helped to shape my outlook on love and relationships. I used to struggle to try to understand why Gracie would tolerate the arrangement, or why, a woman as beautiful as she, who really could have had her pick of men, decided to settle on "man sharing". More clear to me is the perspective of the many Caribbean wives who decided to look the other way, when their husbands maintained relationships outside of their marriages.

From the earliest colonial period, life in the Caribbean has been tumultuous, and the people have had to endure great poverty and economic hardship. Thus, a woman would opt to stay in a union, despite having an unfaithful husband, because he at least contributed financially to the household.

Back in the day and even now, the men of Caribbean earn far more than women, and this income was especially depended upon by women whose primary responsibility was the well-being of their children.

There is no doubt BoBo benefited from my Grandmother's ability to remain calm, no matter what circumstance, actions, or words were flung at her. Often Gracie held her tongue with BoBo just to keep the peace.

Today, when speaking to friends of my generation I pose the question: "don't we as women have a right to our emotions, to express our hurt, anger, and disappointment? And must those needs and rights always place second to our desires for love and companionship?"

I have concluded Gracie remained in her relationship with BoBo for all those years, assuming the role of a distant "co-wife," because despite its limitations, their bond provided a certain stability, familiarity, and financial assistance.

The truth is, I will never know for sure her reasons for staying with my grandfather, and at this point as she enters into her ninth decade, and with

BoBo long gone, Gracie will never reveal to me or anyone the reason for her choices what it was that kept her going.

The True Story of Great-Gram
By Mariana Williams

I only knew my great-grandmother from pictures and speaking on the phone a few times but she was always remembered lovingly when the Swedish side of my family gathered. Everyone focused on two attributes: "Gram was the funniest person we ever met," and "Gram was the fattest lady I'd ever seen." My mom would add with a wistful smile, "and I was really proud of that."

Back in the day our family never jumped on airplanes to cross the country and visit Waterbury, Connecticut, where my mom, aunt, and grandma were born. Phone calls were abbreviated flurries of non sequiturs because someone was standing over your shoulder anxiously waiting for their turn to talk. Pricey seconds and minutes ticked away as you strained to hear. Yet, I felt I knew my great-grandmother from her voice and the black and white snapshots—her hair pulled back in a loose bun, wearing an apron, leaning on the railing of her porch on Elm Street. Perhaps it was her crinkle-framed smiling eyes, but I knew that she possessed the one quality that I revered above all others. Gram was said to be hilarious.

How Josephine Terry got to Connecticut was not hilarious. Around 1873, she was born of phantom parents and raised by an aunt and uncle, off an island in Sweden. (I didn't think of Sweden as having an island culture.) What came next are bold facts as tragic as a Dickensian tale, or at the very least, bad luck. I'll present both scenarios.

Uncle was a member of a crew that sailed across the ocean from Sweden a few times a year delivering goods to New York, then up to various ports to Newfoundland. When Josephine was sixteen, she wanted to see the new world, and what teenager wants to be trapped on a rural farm? After running around the hillsides with the goats, wearing a bonnet and snacking on dried herring from an apron pocket, anyone would jump at the chance. Okay, I added that.

I ask you the reader, had Aunt and Uncle tired of the teenager they'd been saddled with? They had no children of their own, perhaps they longed for some peace and quiet around the farm? After all, they did watch over her for sixteen years. Or, did they think how lovely to give Josephine the advantage of seeing New York!

They decided to go. Uncle and Josephine would stay in the regular boarding house in New York where he always went on such trips. After a day or two, as planned, he joined his shipmates and traveled up the coast to Newfoundland, Canada, promising to return in a week.

But Uncle disappears forever. Hmmm, a bad storm? Or, did something unspeakable happen once Uncle and niece were thousands of miles away—causing him to flee? After Newfoundland, did he return to the farmhouse in Sweden, greeting his wife with a shrug? Or, did Uncle heroically fight for his life on a ship that went down in the cold Atlantic? Was he muttering phrases in a lifeboat, half delirious and weeping for the poor, abandoned and innocent Josephine left in the boarding house without money to pay for the week?

Now she's alone in the new world with no chance of returning home. Bad luck? Or, was it by design? At sixteen, she was on her own without knowing a soul, without papers, money, or the ability to speak English.

The boarding house owner was not one to take pity on the girl. She quickly put a broom in her hand and made her an indentured servant. Josephine met another Swedish girl in the neighborhood, who worked for a rich family and offered to teach Josephine how to cook. My great Gram was a quick study and found a job cooking for a moderately wealthy family in New York. I guess things heated up in the kitchen and she dished out some sweets, because she turned up pregnant. To his credit, the son of the house married the hilarious, good cook and they had four children. My grandmother, Marian Louise Terry, told us what we know today of her mother.

This can hardly be a happy ending because, according to my mother and aunt, their grandfather, Josephine's husband, always sulked in the basement with books and a pipe and never spoke to my mother and aunt their entire life. He was a grouch to the nth degree. Probably seeing himself as an intellectual, he envisioned his life as clipped short by his immigrant wife who had no command of the language and put on the pounds. My mom and aunt lived in fear of their grandfather and never met his parents. John Terry's family disowned him for his dalliance.

Gram had lifelong friends and children who adored her. Who cares if there's a grouch in the basement sucking a pipe and brooding over what might have been? To this day, the things I care about most are all upstairs, delicious food and lots of laughs.

How Mom-Mom Became My Mom
By Terri Scott

Mom-Mom used to celebrate my birthdays like they were national holidays. One would think since my birthday commonly fell around Easter time it would get lost in the festivities, much like my Christmas-born younger brother's birthday did.

But Mom-Mom would never allow it. I have too many photos of me in my party dresses, surrounded by Easter baskets and Easter bunnies, proving the real star of the Easter season was little ole me. That's just how things were after Mom-Mom became one of my mothers.

She wasn't much older than I am now when she became my grandmother at forty-four years old. Looking back from a vantage point of maturity, she was old enough to be my grandmother, although my 16 year-old mother clearly wasn't old enough for her role in my life. It only made sense baby Terri would need another parent. Since my teenaged mother was still attending high school and was living at home, I was born into a family already equipped with two mothers.

Amazingly, I still remember the official moment when Mom-Mom came to be. I was around three years old, and the three of us Benjamin women were crammed into my grandmother's small, straight-out-of-the-70s kitchen. She was baking a potato while having a conversation with my natural mother.

I was at my grandmother's leg, trying to get her attention as she tried to keep me from getting burned on the oven door. In the true spirit of my impatience, I wanted my turn to talk to my grandmother. I remember tapping at my grandmother's leg, pleading for attention by mimicking my mother and saying, "Mom, Mom, MOOOOOMMMM!" My grandmother looked down and said, "Don't call me 'Mom', I'm not your mother." Then she paused for a beat and proclaimed, "You can call me Mom-Mom since I'm your grandmother." And so, a life-long label for my grandmother was born.

The years between the Mom-Mom incident and the time when my grandmother brought me back to Philly from living with my parents in South Carolina are fuzzy. It was like my life fast-forwarded from one movie scene to the next. I had a new, full-time official mother who I knew in my mind was my grandmother.

It's funny, most people remember their grandmothers, especially those of my grandmother's generation as being old, stuffy, white haired, and full of kindness and cookies. While my grandmother was full of kindness, she was still a forty-year-old, red-haired, fiery, stylish, on-the-go, on-the-move woman.

Her time serving me as a single mother was short, but I'm amazed at what an impact her parenting has left upon my adult life, now that I'm in my early forties.

I remember mornings of coffee, bagels and Scrapple, a regional breakfast meat. Who knew that Mom-Mom would be responsible for my life-long love for the taste of coffee, whether it was in the mug, the flavor of ice cream and sometimes, the flavor of yogurt?

"You can have just a sip or two, not too much," she said to me the first time I sampled coffee out of her morning mug. Taking "just a sip or two" became a special treat and a respite from my also beloved, yet expected cup of orange juice in the morning. To this day, there's a part of my soul that dances when I smell the intermingled aromas of coffee and bagels together.

My love of a salad with plenty of avocado? Yep, Mom-Mom was responsible for that, too. I remember her dieting phase and how salad and soup were our dinner guests for a time. She'd always slice off a piece of avocado for me to sample before chopping them into the salad. She'd collect those round pits in a jar.

"I can use these in the soil of my plants," she said. She'd also collect eggshells for the same purpose.

And, God knows the woman had a green thumb! There was an ivy plant in her front vestibule area, stretching from one end of the ceiling to the next. I also remember the elephant ear plant she kept shiny with dabs of mayonnaise. There were hanging spider plants, too. Her in-home bounty was only a hint of the harvest she had growing in the backyard.

To this day, I've never tasted tomatoes as juicy and fresh as Mom-Mom's. I'm so grateful that I've experienced the difference between store-bought tomatoes and backyard-fresh tomatoes. There's no comparison, and believe me, I've tried to find the same sweet tasting tomatoes whenever I make my grocery runs.

Mom-Mom trained my taste buds for fresh tomatoes by picking one off the vine, slicing it in half with a knife, sprinkling it with salt, then watching me carefully as I munched with glee.

As one might guess, food still plays an enormous role in my life. How could it not when Mom-Mom invented the food-reward relationship in my life? For example, Friday afternoons were reserved for McDonald's as my treat after a long, hard week of first grade.

Those late 1970s Saturdays with Mom-Mom are what absolutely defined me as a child and well into my teen and adult years. Saturdays were for exploration, shopping and dining. Although Philly is one of the largest cities in the U.S., she'd have nothing to do with shopping in Center City on Saturday.

I won't repeat what she'd say about the average black person who shopped at the Gallery Mall on Saturdays, but it's suffice to say even though we were African Americans ourselves, Mom-Mom felt her dignity and sanity were better protected at the malls and higher-end shopping centers in the well-to-do suburban towns surrounding Philly.

"You need to learn how to associate with people who aren't like you," she'd admonish me. "You can't learn anything by hanging around the same people all the time. That's the problem with black people! They don't want to be around anyone else, they want to shop in the same neighborhoods, they want to eat the same food, with their damned greasy fried chicken, cheese steaks, and fried rice from the corner store all the damned time."

My grandmother also taught me how to shop, and by that I mean how to make my pennies cry out for mercy in the most dignified manner possible.

"I don't shop at Salvation Army with their old funky clothes," she'd sniff in disgust. "I go to those consignment shops and the thrift stores where the rich people go. Hell, they wear something once and then they're through with it. Hey, that's good news for me!"

She'd continued, "Let them get rid of their stuff after only one time. Terri, did you know that sometimes they leave the tags on the clothes they give away?"

This act was absolutely unheard of in our working-class world. We wore everything we bought, and we rarely donated anything.

"So, why not take advantage?" she'd proclaim, tilting her head slyly for emphasis. This began my life-long practice of looking like a million while only spending a few bucks. Mom-Mom's homes were full of clothing and furniture pieces worth thousands of dollars, although I'd be shocked if everything retailed at hundreds of dollars, the way she shopped!

Many kids grew up believing that their parents' statements are edicts to be believed and trusted for a lifetime. While Mom-Mom was parenting me, she made her share of incendiary statements and yet, she taught me one of the best life lessons; the art of knowing when to keep your mouth shut, especially if it pertained to opinions about others.

"Be careful what you say around folks, Terri. You don't know who's related to who, or who is friends with who," she'd warn me.

She made other proclamations I learned to tune out (because she also taught me to think for myself). But one of the last lessons she passed on to me is one that I will believe for as long as I live, especially now that I'm almost the age that she was when she became my grandmother.

I was 20 years old, standing on her steps, tuning her out as she nagged at me about everything she could think of at the time. Our relationship had vastly deteriorated by this time for a variety of reasons. However, since she was such a good parent to me in my early years, I had the good sense to keep my mouth shut as she nagged.

She took a step back, looked up at me on the steps and made the proclamation of a lifetime: "You know, God doesn't give you youth and wisdom at the same time!"

How I wish I could go back to my younger self and scream it to myself, "Listen to her!" I would have saved myself so many years of self-inflicted misery.

What I really wish, is time could have stood still. I wish I could have her with me again. But every time I look in the mirror examining my increasingly aging face, she's present. She's not here, but she's with me.

She's in the smile and the eyebrows that I've inherited from her. She's in the auburn color of my hair strands in the summertime. She's present with me every time I'm forced to buy a specialty-sized bra. I hear her voice telling me when it's time to "Buy a nice coat!" whenever I see a fabulous coat hanging up in Burlington Coat Factory.

No, she's no longer around. But, despite my best efforts to leave my past in the past, I'll always have my second mother's imprint on my life.

The Secret of the Hankie
By Wendy Tanzer

After my grandmother's funeral, I remained in town for a couple of weeks to grieve and reconnect and heal with family. The only "out-of-towner," I agreed to stay in Grammy's house, conveniently making myself part of the action while my sister and brother-in-law, three nephews, two cousins and their families came and went; each of us working to organize, agonize and rhapsodize over the flotsam and jetsam of a ninety-five year life.

Several long days of coffee and telling "Grammy stories" later, we had worked our way through most of the house. One evening, after the entire family had shared a casual and amiable meal, I had the house to myself. I poured a glass of Chardonnay and climbed two flights of stairs to the attic – the final bastion of undisturbed treasures.

And there it was: The old steamer trunk where Grammy kept all the clothes and jewels we used for playing "dress-up" together. I pulled the two sides apart and was immediately cradled in the familiar, musty odor. In the third drawer, I found my grandmother's linen handkerchief. Instantly, I was transported back to a delicious childhood and into the big, stuffed chair where Grammy and I spent story time, every Sunday.

"Grammy what's that?" I was staring at the lace showing just below the crook of her elbow, from the arm of her sweater.

"My sweet girl… it's a hankie. Ladies always keep a hankie in their sleeve." Grammy pulled out a fresh, crisp, linen handkerchief finished with delicate lace and a hand-embroidered monogram. In the corner was a little yellow spot. I must have looked confused because she explained,

"That's my cologne. I put a drop on my hankie so I always smell good." She smiled down at me.

I looked back into her warm, loving, blue eyes and was spellbound. I asked, "But Grammy, what's the hankie for? You don't really blow your nose in it, do you?"

"Oh, no!" She laughed. "This one's for show, not for blow!" Then she pulled me close and taking the linen handkerchief in her hand, she lowered her voice to a whisper. "I'm going to tell you a lady-secret." Holding her hankie flat, she said, "First, you fold it in four, like so. Then you fold it again into a triangle shape." She demonstrated each step as she went. "See how all the lace is together now?" Grammy waited, holding the hankie for my inspection.

I nodded eagerly. I just knew this was a super-important lady-secret and with the intensity only a little girl can muster, I watched her every move.

"You tuck the point up into your sleeve so that only the lace peeks out." The beautiful folds of lace rested perfectly on her forearm. "It shows that you know how to be a well-dressed lady. That's what this pretty hankie is for." She pulled a tissue from her pocket. "Here is the one I use when I need to blow my nose!" She gave a laugh.

But I was still trying to wrap my mind around the lace. "Are you going out, Grammy? Can I come, too?"

"No, I'm not going anywhere. I'm staying right here with you." She squeezed me tight.

"Why do you have the hankie in your sleeve?"

"I always have a hankie in my sleeve, Sweet Girl. I wouldn't be a fit grandmother if I didn't. That's what ladies do."

Pulled from my reverie back into the here and now, I drew the hankie to my face and breathed deeply. Yardley English Lavender. Had anyone asked, I would have sworn to it.

I folded, then tucked her handkerchief into my sleeve, just as I'd been taught so many years before, smiling at the memory – and at my grandmother's grace. I thought about my own grown daughter who had probably never even heard of such a ritual. Would she (or could she) appreciate the subtlety and allure it represented? Modern motherhood didn't permit such lessons in feminine wiles. My family would have considered it sexist. I shook my head.

Closing the trunk, I vowed to share "the secret of the hankie" with my granddaughters when the time comes. I looked up and said, "I'll always remember. I promise. I love you, Grammy."

Don't Tell Joe
By Robyn Segal

"Don't tell Joe," she said on the phone.

"I won't," I reassured my Nana.

A check had arrived in the mail earlier that day, a gift from Nana. Joe was my grandfather, well, step-grandfather. Nana was always sending me checks: money for winter coats, long distance phone bills, birthdays, holidays, and replacement windows for my first house. I never knew when I was getting a check until she called me, sometimes just a day after she mailed it. She always warned me, "Don't tell Joe."

"Did you get the check? I hope it didn't get lost in the mail," she would say.

Then she would ask me to check the mailbox while she waited on the phone.

She'd remind me, "When you get it, call me, but don't tell Joe."

"Don't tell Joe" was our code. Without explanation, I understood that Joe was not to know about the new shoes she'd bought me, the winter coat and especially those replacement windows.

I never understood the nuances of telling Joe or not telling Joe. I only understood that my Nana wanted the gifts she sent to me to be a secret, our secret.

Sometimes the checks were from both Nana and Joe, and she would blurt out in the middle of our phone calls,

"You forgot to thank Joe for the check."

She would then abruptly hand the phone over to Joe and I would thank him for the check, a check I didn't even know was from him.

It wasn't just the gifts that she wanted me to hide from Joe; there were other things, all seemingly arbitrary. I just left my job, "Don't tell Joe." I'm getting married, "Don't tell Joe." I'm gay, "Don't tell Joe."

Thus, Joe was largely left in the dark. Though, always friendly and eager to hear what was happening in my life, my grandmother controlled our conversations with her eyes. They would dart around the room giving her face a kind of crazed look. Without a word, Nana's eyes screamed one thing: Don't say anything, Joe might find out.

My Nana saw everything as a secret. If I was visiting her sister, my Aunt Lilly, she would remind me to not talk about my mother.

If I was visiting my mother, I was sworn to not to tell her about cousin Sherman.

My grandmother was paranoid. Keeping all those secrets gave her plenty to worry about. What if Joe found out that I had switched my college major or worse, that my mother was going back to school? These were the things that kept my Nana up at night. Absent of her worries, she would have nothing to do.

She kept Joe in a kind of insulated bubble, largely ignorant of the details of our lives. He would often ask how things were going with my job; then he would look completely lost. No one had told him that I left that job two years earlier.

As Nana's chauffeur, Joe mostly took us shopping and was often forced to wait in the car, alone, reading the paper. He never asked why he couldn't come in the store with us. I, for one, was grateful. In his presence there was very little Nana and I could discuss. It was easier to visit Nana without Joe present. At least then I could talk.

At home she would often send him on a fool's errand, finding any reason to get him out of the house. "Joey, can you pick up some grapefruit juice and that cereal I like?" she'd say.

Once Joe was gone, Nana would start asking me questions: the kind of questions you just couldn't ask around

Joe, like "Did the shoes fit?" "Did you buy the new bra?" or "What about that haircut?"

Joe was a nice guy and I never thought he would care if my new shoes fit but some wire had tripped in Nana's head. She started suspecting Joe of doing things, stuff he shouldn't have been doing, things like saying "hello" to the lady downstairs. He nodded at the lady as he and Nana got into their car. Joe made the apparent mistake of holding the door open when the lady's hands were full of groceries.

Then Nana suspected him of spending too much time in the bathroom. She started to confide her suspicions to my mother, later to my uncle, and finally she broke down, confiding in me. She made it sound so believable. She was so convincing. After all, anything was possible. She suspected that Joe was talking to the lady through the toilet. It was a clandestine affair, communicated through a series of flushes and love notes scribbled on toilet paper.

Poor Joe tried to defend himself, but Nana just wouldn't let it go. After all, he still needed to use the bathroom. It was soon after that we took her to the local mental hospital. She resisted at first, but ultimately settled into a nice little cottage on the grounds of Long Island Jewish Psychiatric Hospital. When I went to visit her, she was no longer talking about Joe and the toilet; she was calling out for her mother, screaming "Mama" as I tried to calm her down.

Nana was ultimately discharged from the mental facility, and soon after she became unhinged again and attacked the neighbor (the lady she thought Joe was having an affair with) in the parking lot. My Nana was a strong woman. I can imagine her swinging her "Public Television" tote bag at the woman's head.

Management evicted Nana and Joe from their apartment. Who could blame them? Joe broke down without Nana and both he and Nana were placed in locked units at different mental hospitals. Somehow they were both too in love to stay together. They had to be separated.

We put their belongings in storage, and later when they were better, my mother found a residential hotel for them. Nana seemed back to her old self, but Joe was broken by the whole experience and took to the bed. Nana seemed perfectly content in her new surroundings and with Joe in bed all the time she could keep an eye on him and enjoy the freedom of saying whatever she liked.

Nana and I would chat for hours while Joe lay in the bed groaning that he wanted to die. Nana was unfazed. As for the rest of the family, we were all somewhat relieved. As long as Joe stayed in bed, Nana could trust him and they could remain together. She still sent me those checks and always admonished me, "Don't tell Joe."

Joe stayed in bed for three years. My Nana made a life for herself at that residential hotel, made friends with the other residents and made Joe's meals every day.

Without notice or warning, one day, Joe got up and out of bed. He once again was a jolly guy who sang Broadway tunes in his robust baritone voice. She didn't come out and say it, but I could tell Nana wasn't so happy to have the old Joe back. Living in that hotel presented numerous possibilities for Joe to carry on with the women there, through the building's many toilets.

Joe was ready to reclaim his life. Just as suddenly as he took to the bed he got up, found a realtor and rented them a new apartment. Things weren't perfect but they remained together until Joe died years later.

When it became evident that Joe was dying, I asked Nana when I should come to visit him one last time. By then, he was in the final stages of cancer and we knew the end was near. She discouraged me from coming. There was nothing left to not tell Joe, but still, she could never be sure.

Surrogate Grandmother
By Chelsea Uchytil

My grandmother gave birth to me and my twin brother Chad. She was Arlette Swietzer, the first woman in the United States to be a surrogate grandmother. Although it made news around the world it is normal to us, because my mom was born without a uterus. It's difficult to try to explain my twin Chad and my relationship with our Grandma. I know Grandma was my Mom's surrogate. All our lives we have known Grandma carried us in her, "stomach," not our mom.

How we got here never made a difference. It was normal to us. No one in our family makes a big deal of it, or even mentions it.

Maybe that's why we are so close. It's just so natural for us. Our friends all know our story and they love my grandparents as well as they do our parents.

We've had countless sleepovers at their house since we were little. They were like our second parents. Every weekend in middle school my best friend Lexie would pack a bag and bring it to school. Grandpa would pick us up for the weekend and bring us back to town on Sunday. Even during our high school years we still spent much of our time out at their place. Chad and I continue to spend a lot of time at our grandparent's home. It is the gathering place for all six of us grandkids. Their forest home was, and still is, our paradise.

Grandma and Grandpa and I share quite a unique relationship. I see them almost daily, and if I don't, we exchange many texts, emails, and phone calls. I love sharing even the smallest things that happen in my life with them. Grandma is definitely my sounding board for when I need to get something off my chest. Whether or not I'm in the wrong, she is always so good about just hearing what I need to say and giving the best advice she sees fit. I am so blessed to have them both. They are such an important factor in my life, words could never explain.

Grandma has always been extra worrisome for our well-being (for the other grandkids also). When Chad and I would stay out there on the weekends with friends and go hiking for a couple of hours, Grandpa would send us off with the dogs and a, "Have fun!" While Grandma had a list of precautions to be careful; carry a large stick, make lots of a noise, and a reminder of what poison ivy looked like. Grandma actually wrote a small children's book of how, "Grandma worries about everything and Grandpa worries about nothing." Grandpa enjoys telling how when Chad and I had our first prom, she woke up in the middle of the night and grabbed the phone answering, "Chad? Chelsea?"

To which Grandpa replied, "What are you doing? The phone didn't even ring." It just goes to show it isn't how you get here that's important, it is where you are going and love of family that matters most.

My Little Dutch Baby
By Roy Barnes

It is nighttime and I lay alone in a large bed. The pink bedspread keeps me warm, but is dotted with little white prickly points that make my skin itch. The moonlight shines onto the south wall of my sleeping quarters, making a picture of London Bridge at dusk-time clearly visible. The trees rumble against the roof. This disturbance sounds as if the household is being intruded upon by burglars or ghosts. I am frightened enough to jump out of the bed, turn the lights on, and go to the living room to sleep on the couch. This is a scene from my childhood, repeated again and again in the home of my late grandmother, Emma Denney.

The fears I sometimes experienced during the night in my grandparents' home were at least an escape from the realities of the far from perfect, lower class family I found myself trapped in. Grandma and Grandpa Denney possessed an immaculate home and furnishings compared to what my mom and dad had acquired. My grandparents' ability to afford the extras that consumerism had to offer gave me the incentive to visit there often. I managed to cipher most of the toys and fast food I craved from them, much to the chagrin of my parents.

The two most notable physical characteristics that my grandmother possessed were her petite height and size, barely scaling five feet and one hundred pounds. She also had a large nose, a trait from the Dutch side of her family. One afternoon, I started calling her "My Little Dutch Baby," while hugging her affectionately on the living room couch.

The days I remember most with my grandmother would begin with my grandpa being sent off to work after a hearty breakfast and a quick kiss to his job at the Board of Public Utilities. He maintained the water lines for the city of Casper, Wyoming. Since my grandma and I would have a busy day ahead, she admonished me to wash my hands and face so we could get into her Plymouth sedan en route to her monthly chores of going around town to pay bills. After that, we'd do some afternoon grocery shopping at her favorite Albertson's store in the Hilltop Shopping Center, which she dubbed "the commissary."

She always dressed up to go out, and looked especially nice when she donned her black turtleneck sweater that went well with a gold-plated medallion she often wore around her neck. It was a pair of praying hands. My grandmother carried herself with a graceful walk that introduced a charmed elegance to those with whom she came into contact.

McDonald's or Colonel Sanders was the usual lunchtime fare between bill paying and marketing. After some of the Colonel's Original Recipe or a Big Mac and fries, we'd grocery shop. Ninety per cent of the time, I'd get some kind of replica police gadget as we came down the toy aisle. I got to choose TV dinners and the frozen pizza-type snacks I was hungry for, as well as any sweets that tickled my fancy. For dinnertime she usually bought some round steak, chicken, and pork chops that would go well with the frozen packages of cut-up potatoes that would eventually be fried or baked. One time I talked her into buying me some shark meat, as I wanted to experience the novelty of eating something exotic and expensive. She protested that I wouldn't like the taste of this delicacy. Come dinnertime, I slowly and torturously ate two bites of the beast she pan-fried. Then I pushed the plate of shark meat toward the center of the table in disgust.

I often accompanied my grandmother to the Werner Wildlife Museum to look at the taxidermy exhibits of big game, and to the restored nineteenth century outpost called Fort Caspar, which predated the founding of the city of Casper in 1888. The city name is spelled differently than the historical landmark's nomenclature for reasons that aren't clear. She loved to take photographs of the fort's Old West memorabilia and/or of me in front of some frontier motif display with her compact, box-shaped Kodak camera.

In the mid-1970s, my grandmother was diagnosed with diabetes. She took medication every day, diligently checking the labels of everything she ate and drank to make sure very little or no sugar was contained in the products. It frustrated me that she couldn't eat an ice cream cone with me or even something like ketchup, because the condiment contained too much sugar for her strict diet. Grandma Denney always worried about getting cut because her blood clotting system took longer than a non-diabetic person's to halt the bleeding, even if she just sustained a minor scratch.

I found my Grandma Denney's eccentricities very amusing. As a devout Christian, she preached to me about the decadence of rock and roll. But going against her own rhetoric, she would listen to KTWO on a daily basis. It featured hits from stars like Paul McCartney and the Starland Vocal Band, whose hit song called "Afternoon Delight," contained sexual innuendos. Such musical creations blared through the grease-stained GE Portable AM radio in her kitchen, even though she never sang along with the music.

Grandma Denney also went on and on about Johnny Carson, calling him an "evil sinner." Yet almost always before her 11 p.m. bedtime, she'd sit in front of the black and white to watch Johnny's monologue while I engaged in my last bit of horseplay for the evening. Maybe she felt like a captive audience to "The Prince of Late Night Television" because the Denneys of South Jackson Street never opted to get cable; as a result, only one local channel was available for watching after the ten o'clock news. My grandmother would never miss the weatherman's end of day report, ritualistically recording the official temperature and precipitation statistics for Casper in her red notebook.

Peddlers at the door, no matter what they were selling, were rarely turned away by Grandma Denney, especially when children were selling candy or magazines. She would usually give those purchases to the members of my family. Even the Jehovah's Witnesses were invited in and she tried to convert them to her way of thinking when it came to worshipping and serving God.

Every major piece of furniture in the Denney home had a crocheted cover on it, thanks to her love of the hobby. Half of my parent's tables featured her crafted afghans, making my less than ideal home, roughly a mile away, look more presentable to company. She tried to get me to learn the art, but I lost interest after stitching only a few of the knots that made up her intricately designed and multi-colored creations. While working on her patterns, Grandma Denney would often talk about her childhood during The Great Depression. She even confided in me that her first husband, a cruel German man, had kept Adolf Hitler in his house for several months after the war in Europe had been won by the Allies. I was skeptical of this claim but never said a word after she swore me to secrecy, lest the FBI would find out and come take her away.

Both my grandparents had been party animals until their late thirties when they found Jesus one night at a traveling tent meeting. From that time on, they dedicated themselves to being devout Christians. Like an old time evangelist, my grandma warned me against cussing, saying I would be zapped by The Almighty if I did it again. Posters with biblical verses from Oral Roberts' ministry were hung on the bedroom and living room walls in the Denney household. Trinkets like Roberts' replica Tulsa Prayer Tower sat on my grandma's knickknack shelf.

My father on the other hand, didn't wear his religious beliefs on his sleeve and never really got along with my grandma. He often quipped to me, "Roy, your grandma is a religious fanatic."

He accused his mother-in-law of trying to undermine his relationship with my mom from the moment they first started dating, which was only for a month before they got married. My father was twenty-five and had been briefly hitched twice before. My mother hadn't even finished high school and was months from her eighteenth birthday. My dad often repeated how Grandma Denney told my mother, "I don't want you to marry that cab driver."

According to my father, she would even run down his mother, a snuff-dipper who lived in the boondocks of northeast Arkansas. Emma Denney deemed snuff-dipping a "filthy habit," even as she took long drags from her cigarettes.

After visits with my grandparents, I would often cause a lot of trouble back home for at least two days, complaining to my mom about how good it was with them. I had more freedom to do and get what I wanted. My father drove an eighteen wheeler coast to coast, so I had many opportunities to bitch at my mother. I didn't protest too much about the advantages of staying with grandma and grandpa when my dad was home, as I feared getting a whippin.

Gradually, my grandma started refusing to go to the doctor except to get her diabetes medication refilled. In April of 1983, my mother demanded my grandma go to the doctor after she had fallen ill and was extremely weak. Over the next several weeks, she would get progressively worse as cancer ate away much of her being. The last time I saw my grandmother alive was in late May. She was rolling around in her hospital bed, talking incoherently, oblivious to me. My mother had told me she wasn't going to get any better, and I expected her to die. During her final days, I had a recurring dream which gave me hope: It was of my grandma and grandpa walking out of the hospital hand in hand.

But that dream didn't come true. She died on June 7, 1983, one month after her sixty-fourth birthday. I still think about her a lot.

Not everyone can say that they had a special grandmother. But I'm thankful to God that I can.

She Floats Inside My Head
By Vanessa Raney

Once, in the middle of summer, I opened a closet door and saw a huge hulking spider lurking in the shadows above the top shelf. I let out a loud scream, as it was almost the size of my head!

My Grandma came rushing in, noted the size of the creature and hurried to get a broom, returning to kill it with a hard thrust. She must have thrown it away afterwards, but I have no memory of that. I only remember how she rescued me in her home where I spent my early summers.

The summer of the gargantuan spider, though, also brought my duckling trauma. That story, however, is not for the squeamish, or for those quick to decide about serial killers.

Of course I was a messed up child, bottling up anger from things about which I had every right to be angry. Even so, I cannot explain what prompted my actions, why I took the duck and repeatedly slammed it against the wall until it died, its guts spilled out all over the floor.

Yet, the moment it stopped moving, I cried uncontrollably. I knew, at the deepest level, that what I had done was wrong; instantly, too, I felt that no amount of remorse would bring the animal back.

My Grandma, on the other hand, offered no admonishments or asked any questions. Instead, she collected the duck's corpse and threw it away.

To someone else, her actions may not have been enough. What they taught me, though, was that it was okay to be angry; but that acting in anger can lead to bad consequences which cannot always be undone.

Her non-judgment continued at the next turn when, the following summer, we went to the local market and she bought me three colored chicks in blue, red and standard yellow. Yet, for very different reasons, they, too, did not survive.

One I accidentally killed while walking on a log, the chick on the ground beside me; I stepped on it when I slipped. Another died at the fault of a neighbor girl at whom I screamed at the top of my lungs. As for the third chick, my grandmother suggested a stray cat had eaten it, since it had vanished from the backyard where the chicks had been kept.

Thus, given my poor track record, you might be surprised to learn that my Grandma had yet to give up. With the next summer came my brave calico kitten Flowers.

My Grandma, though, had to fight for me to have her. Of the three kittens her neighbor let me play with in the cupola, Flowers was the one I wanted. Then, while waiting outside the front door, I overheard them in conversation; as it turned out, my little dream had been promised to someone else. I almost cried thinking I would lose her.

Instead, I played with her, watched her eat real chicken and drink her milk, worried after her the morning my Grandma left her in the wash bin while she was out getting groceries (I was still asleep when she left), and chastised her for peeing on me when I picked her up from the front garden to bring her inside. This, then, is how my grandmother impressed upon me the value and necessity of second chances—that, while mistakes may happen, they are not by themselves a reason to give up.

Unfortunately, those months with Flowers were also the last summer I spent with my Grandma. Yet it was Alzheimer's, not death that caused our separation; still, she always remembered me the few times we spoke on the phone. That is how I learned that Flowers had run away; I've since had no more pets.

That news, though, also contributed to my decision to stop all contact with my Grandma; once I made it clear that I did not even want to know if she should die, I stopped talking with her and refused to hear any more about her. Of course I had moments when I grieved at the possibility of her death; but I did not want to think of her dead.

Yet she floats inside my head like a spirit who's always with me. In early 2015, she died for real.

Never Lose Faith
By Pat St. Pierre

Several months ago I had trouble with my washing machine. I had to lug clothes to the Laundromat. Ugh, that was a terrible task! Today my dishwasher broke. Here I am with dishes galore and no dishwasher!

When I called my husband at work, he said, "You better call the repairman right away tomorrow. You don't want to wash dishes by hand."

"I sure don't," I answered.

I felt thankful that my husband sympathized with me. Feeling less sorry for myself, I sat down to enjoy a cup of tea. I started thinking about familial assistance and support groups. Where would we be without them? I reminisced about my grandmother and the type of life that she had led. Would she be complaining like I am, I asked myself? No, she certainly wouldn't. Her expression "Never lose faith, for after midnight a new day will begin," came into my mind.

How different my grandmother's life was from mine. She married young and had her first child at 15 years of age. A year later she had her second child. Shortly thereafter, her husband left her in Italy while he went to establish a home for her and the children in the United States. Just when she was ready to join him their first son died. How horrible it must have been to bury a child and then leave him behind. After she made the long journey to the States, she then had to try and put her thoughts behind her. There was no emotional support from her husband and no support groups for her. Today she would have had access to support groups for a miscarriage as well as for the death of a child.

A few years later, my grandfather died of pneumonia, leaving my grandmother alone with five children to take care of. She became the sole breadwinner of her family. She provided for her children by raising vegetables, canning, selling milk and eggs, and going to work as a nanny. After her job, she had to come home and tend the garden, milk the cows, collect the eggs and care for her family. She made sure that her children did not go on welfare. She was proud of herself and always felt that as long as one did "honest" work you never had to be ashamed.

My grandmother scrimped and saved on her small earnings. When her children got married, she was able to give each of them a parcel of land on which to build a house. How many of us today can afford to give our children land on which to build a house?

Her enthusiastic spirit continued throughout her life. She supported herself and tackled any task that confronted her. No one ever heard her complain no matter how rough things got. I remember one day when I was driving home from seeing a friend, I saw my grandmother walking along the road. I stopped and picked her up.

When she got into my car I asked her, "Why didn't you take the bus or ask someone to drive you?"

Years of determination were etched on her face. "I wouldn't spend the money for the bus and everyone was busy," she answered firmly. "I didn't want to miss my meeting so I walked the ten miles."

Today most of us complain when we have to drive to the supermarket and then go to the cleaners. What if we had to walk to those places?

My grandmother lived in a foreign country without relatives and community support groups. No one came to her aid to help ease the pain after her child and her husband died. When depression set in there was no one in which to confide. She had to rely on her inner conscience to help heal her pain and allow her to face the next day.

From my grandmother's strength a strong foundation has been built. How proud she would be today to know that her children have all been successful and have increased their wealth. Her grandchildren and great grandchildren are attending college and making a better life for themselves.

So, as I sit here and think about my broken dishwasher I also think about the kind of life I have with all modern-day conveniences and the support of family members and community groups.

I jump up from my chair without hesitation as I hear my grandmother's words "never lose faith." With that thought in mind I pile the dishes into the dishpan and wash them, for tomorrow is indeed a new day.

Memories of My Grandma:
Buttons and Buses
By Lynn Jarrett

She never held a job a day in her life. She never drove a car or had a driver's license. She only had a high school education. She lived half her life with severe, crippling rheumatoid arthritis so bad she could not straighten her fingers. But, she did make the world's best macaroni and cheese and the sweetest peach cobbler. And she had the most outstanding collection of buttons in a tin hidden away in her closet. Best of all, Grandma let me take out the tin and play with her buttons whenever I wanted. My Grandma and I had a special bond, we even have the same name.

One of the favorite memories I have of her has to do with deer hunting season. Wait! I know what you are thinking, but no, neither of us were deer hunters. My Dad and Grandpa were the big game hunters in the family. Every November, they traveled to a hunting club about sixty miles away to spend a week. Grandma was afraid to stay by herself, but did not want to leave her house vacant to come and stay with us, due to crime on the rise in her neighborhood.

Being the dutiful granddaughter, I would go stay with her even though I was in the eighth grade and still had to attend school. Grandma lived on the opposite side of town from us, so I had to take the city bus to and from school. Grandma would watch me walk down her street to the corner and wait for the bus to come and take me downtown. Before I stepped on to the bus, I would look back and wave. She smiled a warm smile and waved back to me until the bus pulled off. Once I got downtown, I took a second bus eastbound to my junior high school.

After school, I retraced my path back to Grandma's house. As soon as I stepped off the bus at the corner of her street, I could see her standing on the front porch, a big smile on her face. Even though it meant I had to get up earlier in the morning to get to school on time, it was a small price to pay, because during that time I had Grandma all to myself. I will always cherish those special times we had together and I have her buttons to prove it!

Movies with Nana
by MK McFadden

At eight years old, I spent the summer for the first and last time with my Nana in Florida. I am her youngest granddaughter, the fifth grandchild out of seven. Our relationship was good but I was reaching the age where I was too cool to be treated like a baby.

Nana lived in Fort Lauderdale, in a corner apartment with a white kitchen and large windows where the morning sun poured in. My aunt and cousins lived not far away and we spent our days at the beach baking in the sun, and by the time I went back home, I was shades darker than my usual chestnut colored skin.

When it was too hot, our plans changed. Instead of the shore, we'd eat Pop Tarts and head to the movies. Nana lived near a theater that showed old movies for a dollar so we went every day. I don't remember the films that we saw, probably some late 1990s romantic comedies or action films that in hindsight seem awful.

It was my grandmother who taught me to love stories, to watch films that I would normally never pick for myself. She does this even now when I visit her. Nana will choose a movie from Netflix I could never even imagine watching. She adores action movies: *Die Hard* and *Mission Impossible* are more her speed while I love classics like *2001: A Space Odyssey*. Her choices are a nice change of pace and a reminder to widen my boundaries. In fact because of Nana, I wound up in film school where I received my Bachelor's degree in cinema studies.

Soon after my visit, my Nana left Fort Lauderdale and moved back to my hometown, so we were able to keep up our tradition of seeing dollar movies. The movie house in South Carolina was just a few minutes away from our house and we would go see sometimes two films in a weekend. The theater was run down, with ripped seats and sticky floors. It's the kind of place you would expect to see in horror film, yet it really exists.

While my friends were hanging out in the neighborhood, I was sitting in a darkened room with my Nana staring at a big silver screen on the edge of my seat, eating chips and Gummy Bears.

Nana and I had our system down pat. I would buy the tickets except for the features rated "PG-13" or "R" because the manager would practically conduct a police investigation if you looked too young, so Nana bought those. We would try to get to the movies early to get great seats, sometimes even packing dinner and taking it with us to make sure we got there on time. My Mom would occasionally join us, but most of the time it would be just Nana and me watching action movies, cheering on Tom Cruise or Bruce Willis.

Our tradition continued through middle and high school, and even during my college breaks. One of the last films we saw together was a horror film, which at the end I turned to her and said, "This is the loudest movie I have ever seen." Nana smiled and nodded in agreement.

My memories of sitting next to Nana, giggling and whispering at the movies enthralled by the magic of Hollywood are remembrances I will cherish for a lifetime.

Nowadays, Nana and I don't watch a lot of films at the theatre because we have the luxury of Netflix and films we can watch at home. I still get lots of phone calls from her asking me if I have heard of some movie or another and urging me to see a hit everyone's talking about.

It's beautiful the way technology has allowed us to continue our tradition of enjoying our favorite pastime. We still talk endlessly about movies we'll never forget and the ones we hated. It's a bond of love of entertainment and make-believe and it will never be broken.

I think I'll give Nana a call now. Maybe we can watch a movie together over the phone.

Grandma's Special Ingredient
By Jacqueline Seewald

I never knew much about my own grandmothers. But my husband Monte's maternal grandmother, Grandma Ethel, was quite an amazing woman. I'll never forget the life lessons she taught me.

My husband was the oldest grandchild and very close to his grandparents, so it was quite natural I would get to know Grandma Ethel rather well. When Monte and I were first married I was especially grateful for Grandma Ethel and her wisdom. Even if she was quite mysterious.

Everything she did was done with exactness and perfection. Every pot in her kitchen gleamed. There was never a speck of dirt or dust in her apartment. And although they never had much money, the apartment and furnishings always looked lovely and modern. You would never know that Grandma Ethel, this tiny woman of four feet eleven inches, worked full-time in a factory most of her life, so both her son and daughter could have college educations—debt free.

Grandma Ethel never forgot to send beautiful greeting cards or generous gifts for every member of the family's birthday or anniversary. Her presents were always the most thoughtful and useful. The quilt she gave me at my bridal shower was the most lovely I've ever seen or owned to this day.

She was very interested in the lives of her children and grandchildren, but never interfered or offered unsolicited opinions and advice. She explained this to me once.

"I listen but I don't say anything unless asked. When my son told us he was marrying outside of our religion, I made no comment. I welcomed his wife into the family. They are happy together and that's what matters. All I ever wish is that my children and grandchildren and great grandchildren have good lives."

Grandma Ethel had many talents, too. She was fluent in numerous languages, but she never ignored or looked down on domestic matters. She made her own curtains out of silky aqua blue material that brightened her kitchen windows. She also had a knack for fashion. She even sewed all her daughter's dresses as well as her own.

Grandma Ethel's greatest talent was cooking. She truly had a gift for creating fine meals. As she grew older, Grandma Ethel still created big holiday feasts. There is one dinner I will never forget. As usual, Grandma Ethel had prepared and cooked an outstanding meal. Even the red grapefruit that she placed in front of us was sweet. There wasn't a hint of sourness. It amazed me. How does one make grapefruit sweet? Finally, I just had to ask. I needed to solve the mystery of how this little old lady managed to provide such remarkably outstanding meals.

"Grandma Ethel, how do you do it?"

"Do what?" she smiled.

"All of it. The cooking and baking, for instance. Why is your roast chicken always so succulent? How do you get your honey cake to be so light?"

"Oh, it's nothing special," she said with a characteristically modest shrug.

"But it is special," I persisted. "Is it because you love cooking, cleaning, shopping, sewing?"

"Oh, no," she answered quickly as if to disabuse me of such a notion. "I don't love it. I just work hard at it."

"Why? I mean what is the reason you give so much of yourself to each task?" I really wanted to know.

My husband gave me one of those looks that said: you are pestering my grandmother. But I wanted to understand, to fathom the mystery, the philosophy behind her perfection. I sensed there was much to learn from her. I wanted very much to know.

Grandma Ethel was quiet and thoughtful for a time. "It's like this. I do a lot of things I don't enjoy but are necessary, like peeling onions for instance, or scrubbing the floors. When I do them, I'm thinking about my family. I want everything to be as good as I can make it for them. I just concentrate on how much I love all of them, and so each task becomes important, something I want to do to the best of my ability.

'It's the same with my cooking." she continued. "I put in the extra effort because I want my family to have the best. So I shop with an eye for the very best quality food I can afford. I examine fruits and vegetables to make certain they aren't bruised or wilted. I buy only fresh meats, fish and poultry."

At last I finally understood Grandma Ethel's essence, why she worked so hard and gave so much of herself. Her remarkable cooking and scrumptious meals contained one simple ingredient. It's called love.

A Dream Come True
By Safiulla Rafai
Editor's Note: Safiulla was just 10 years old when he wrote this story in 2013.

My first and only trip with my grandmother is unforgettable. This story began twenty-five years before I was born, when my dad was ten years old, exactly the age I am today. In the early 1980s, my grandmother was having trouble making an important decision, which would have a long lasting impact on her and her seven children. She was deciding whether to take a job in Saudi Arabia, about 5000 miles away from India, or to stay with her family and face the financial difficulty that they were having at that time. The job in Saudi Arabia was to help pilgrims in the city of Mecca do rituals that more than three million people do every year. Many workers in Mecca help pilgrims do the Hajj rituals. There were many expenses involved, so she was nervous about her decision. She asked my dad to read a prayer before he slept, to ask for guidance from God.

It was as if my grandmother knew something might happen. So that night my weary dad, a ten-year-old boy, went to sleep.

The next morning, grandmother asked him, "Did you see a dream?"

My father's answer was a firm "No."

The next morning, my grandmother asked the same question, and again there was the same "No."

However, on the third day, my father experienced a dream my grandmother thought was a sign. In the dream, he, my grandmother, and one of his brothers entered the Grand Mosque through a beautifully decorated door and prayed near the black cube. He also saw some people he didn't know doing the pilgrimage and the ritual of Hajj. Once my grandmother heard of this dream, she immediately decided to go and take the job in Mecca. She left her household of seven children under the care of my great-grandmother. She left and worked in Saudi Arabia and financially helped her family for seven years, returning home after their financial situation improved.

Hajj is one of the five pillars of my religious beliefs and people in Hajj do the act of 'Tawaf'. Tawaf is when a person goes around the large black cube counter-clockwise seven times. It is performed once a year in remembrance of Abraham, Hagar, and Ishmael. The annual pilgrimage brings about three million pilgrims or Hajjis from around the world to Mecca. Males wear two large towels, one above the waist, the other below. During Hajj, people forget social status and pride, and submit to God in prayer. Now imagine three million people wearing the same two towels! Everyone, rich or poor, young or old, look the same. The Hajjis look like a bunch of swarming bees busy moving in a circular pattern around a giant black cube.

In 2010, ten years after my immediate family came to America, we decided to go for this once in a lifetime visit to the Hajj in Saudi Arabia. My grandmother wanted to see us and we planned for her and my grandfather to come from India and join us in Saudi Arabia. We planned for us to go to India, and afterwards, we would return to America.

However, when we reached the international airport, there was a little surprise. One of our family member's visa had already expired and the passport seal had the wrong date. Therefore, we were not able to go. Our grandparents did continue their journey to Saudi Arabia and returned to India.

Back in America, I felt heartbroken because I was not able to meet my grandmother. It was then my father told about the dream he saw when he was a child. He wondered if his dream would ever come true. Later, we came to know that my grandmother was hospitalized to have her uterus removed. I worried about her deteriorating health, and negative thoughts rushed into my mind. These thoughts kept occurring. To my surprise, five months later, my parents decided to try to go to Hajj again! We repurchased the plane tickets and this time, checked visa dates on all passports. With sorrow, knowing that my grandparents would not be joining us, we started our journey again back to Saudi Arabia.

It was a long airplane ride with food and great movies like *The Karate Kid* on the screen on the back of the seats. We arrived at the International airport in Medina, where my aunt (mom's sister) worked as a dentist. With her was a man wearing a 'jubbah', a long shirt, and on his head a type of handkerchief called, a "rumal" which is worn as a sign of respect. He firmly shook my father's hand. This man was a client of my aunt's. He was a great help. In his car, he took us all around the city. He was very talkative to me because it helped him practice his English. Without him, my aunt would have become tired of us because she would have to take all five of us everywhere, in between her hospital duties.

If not for our tour guide, I think, my aunt would have agreed with Benjamin Franklin, who said, "Guests, like fish, begin to smell after three days."

After driving for 30 minutes from the airport on hot and dusty roads in the midst of the desert, we finally arrived at our aunt's house. We planned to stay there and rest for a week before departing to Mecca, about 300 miles away. When I walked in the front door of the house, I smelled sweet candy because my uncle is a distributor for a candy factory. I ate a feast of candy.

We slept for a few hours and when we woke up, we went to roam and shop in the city of Medina. In the city, we attracted more attention than real aliens do. When we visited a perfume store and the store manager overheard us speaking English, something unusual happened. He pulled out some very good smelling perfumes. He gave me two perfumes for free and then told me to give one to our President and keep the other for myself! This is one of the events that caused me to write a letter to President Obama, to which I also received a response.

A week later, we left Medina to go to Mecca in a bus full of other pilgrims. It took us eight hours to reach Mecca. To me, the drive seemed to take much more time because there were hardly any children on the bus other than my brothers. After reaching Mecca, to our surprise we met our grandparents, who had arrived from India! My grandfather works for the Indian government, and the government decided to send him to do a survey on approximately 70,000 people from India to see how they liked the Hajj facilities. He decided to bring my grandmother along with him. Coincidentally, one of my uncles (my father's brother, who was in his dream) also joined as an employee of a travel agency from India. His trip was also unplanned and purely coincidental. It was wonderful.

Unfortunately, my grandmother did not have the physical capability to take on the rituals of the Hajj. My father talked to the hotel management and arranged for a wheelchair. While he gladly pushed the wheelchair and helped my grandmother complete the Hajj rituals, my mother helped her with other needs.

Alongside three million others, we walked over Prophet Abraham's steps and completed the rituals of Hajj. It was a sunny day, about 100 F°. The air smelled of sweet perfume. If I did not lift my head, I got a mild smell of sweat because I was exactly as tall as an average person's armpit!

The day I touched the black cube was a very special one. Its wall and door are made out of pure gold. Only a few people get the opportunity to touch the black cube, given the entire crowd is trying to reach the cube at once.

After finishing all the rituals of Hajj over a period of five days, we sat in front of the holy mosque. We were worn out from the walking. My dad was talking to his mother and brother. He slowly looked up to find an entrance door. He said that something about the entrance was so familiar, even though he had never seen it before. It must have been from his dream.

Soon we all returned to our homes in India and America. Three months later, we learned that my grandmother had developed cancer. After that, there was not a single weekend that went without my brothers and me talking to grandmother.

One day in the evening, my father got a phone call from India, and he immediately started to cry. My mother took us out of the room and left my father to talk on the phone. She told us to have patience and pray for our grandmother. While I was waiting for someone to tell me what had happened, I became tremendously tired and sleepy. I slept on the corner of my bunker bed, and I saw a dream that had a colorful and bright background with purple and orange triangular prisms on the wall. I saw my grandmother saying twice in Urdu, "I am here." The vivid colors, brightness, and my grandmother's white dress really caught me off guard. I woke up suddenly and saw that my dad was not on the phone anymore. It was unbelievable when I came to know that my grandmother had died because she had just come in my dream!

After I learned of her death, I got two similar dreams in the next four days. I especially remember on the third day of Hajj when she had wished me a great, long life. She had touched my head and mumbled a prayer for my peaceful life and success

The importance of the love and affection she showed me makes me always feel loved. Even though the journey I took with her was my first and last one, I am fine with that because I am full of affectionate memories. With the dream I had the day she died, it is as if my grandmother is assuring me that she is fine and enjoying her afterlife.

Tattooed
By Gerard Sarnat, MD

On September 13, 1945, just after World War II ended, Gerard Sarnat got born. I was called Gerry for short. But if you take my name all the way back to the Polish villages my grandparents were from, way back to the Gesundheits and Sarnatzkys, back to before Sarnatzky got shortened by a swamped clerk at Ellis Island and the German Jerrys made Gesundheit super unpopular after World War I and before we got Frenchified; I'm really Gesundheit Sarnatzky.

In Chicago before I was toddling and my parents weren't poor any more, when Zeyde died, we lived with my grandma up three flights of stairs. Bubbe was always there, staring off in the distance, or on the floor feeding *maches herring* to fatten me up, or spoiling her *boychick* on dill pickles, which Mom hated but never summoned the nerve to tell her mother-in-law to stop.

Southside survival, though a Gaelic nickname, gift for gab, and auburn sidecurls; skulking toward the bus after class let out, Irish gangs kicked my ass, called me Girlie and Kike.

My parents were off working, but Bubbe comforted me after I got home. When she held me tight and wore short sleeves, I had a good look and practiced my numbers. If she noticed, she slowly took me off her lap, stood up and silently put on a coat or sweater.

After Bubbe passed, Dad told me what they were called but never said a word about why they were there. What I do know is that I never got any put on my skin. Which wasn't a big deal, since they weren't the rage like when my youngest daughter got one on her neck, which caused me a lot of grief though I bit my tongue. Perhaps just a coincidence, but I became a plastic surgeon, who removed an awful lot of tattoos from which people wanted to move on.

Years later, traveling to Eastern Europe with my wife and grown children and their families, we tried to track down Skidel, the little shtetl where my Bubbe was from. I told them the whole story, the solid red bricks like grade school in Chicago was. It's almost lovely. A bird sings. One grassy railroad track fades toward the horizon. I realized my Bubbe had spent time in a horrible place called Auschwitz.

What I Know For Sure
By Rhi Myfanwy Kirkland

She tells me I remind her of her mother, my grandmother Marie. High, high, praise from my mother since I will never meet my grandmother. All I have are these snippets, traits I have that my mother loves, and the rare anecdote.

Sitting prominently on a shelf behind my mother's desk, is one striking photograph of my grandmother. She was a prim and proper woman in a dress with a high collar, hair pulled up in a bun and calm features, half-smiling, half-serious. She looks like me when I am dressed for an interview.

Mother assures me Grandmother and I would've gotten along so well. We'd have had so much to talk about. Somehow I doubt this. Too much time has passed between the two of us. The woman in the photograph is quite a few decades removed from the world that I occupy. What would she make of me and this strange reality? Would she get my jokes? Would she be stern?

My grandmother was a nurse. I was told she worked in Connecticut before moving to Saskatoon and marrying my grandfather. Family ties and finances were the main motivations for their marriage (This was before Disney movies sold the world the idea of romantic love). My grandfather, who I also never met, was a doctor and a suitable match. His job paid well, enough to cover a nice home and college tuition for my mother and her siblings. Both my grandparents were from Eastern European families, and maintained their old world values when they reached North America.

She tells me that I'm creative just like my grandmother. My fondness for drawing, painting and photography are a link to the past. Perhaps they are a reflection of some genetic trait that is embedded in my DNA. Even this silly desire to become a writer is something my grandmother would've admired, or so I like to think. My grandmother was an artist, a painter mostly. The chemicals she used may have contributed to her death. She was diagnosed with cancer while my mother was in University.

She tells me not to go to art school. My grandmother hated it and I will too. "They wanted to put her into a box and make her fit their particular idea of art," my mother tells me as a cautionary tale.

At least we still have a few of my grandmother's paintings, but not many. My mother's house flooded, destroying most of what my grandmother had created. The art that survived, my grandfather discarded or neglected. Every time my mother talks about her mother's paintings, I hear heartbreak and loss in her voice, as if losing those creations was like losing her mother all over again.

She tells me things in fragments skewed by the years. I know bits and pieces but it's hard to connect the dots. Within the facts and details of my grandmother's life are lost time and sadness. Memories are far from perfect things. I know that my grandmother made sacrifices for her family. I know that she died too soon. I know that my mother misses her. I believe my every brush stroke and pen mark keeps her legacy alive.

Legacy of Sadness and Strength
by Gargi Mehra

My grandmother Monica was a delicate little creature, always draped in a white saree, the way a good Hindu widow should be dressed. Despite being a brilliant student, she had to cut short her studies because her father married her off at age thirteen.

She birthed her first child at fourteen, followed up with two more kids in the next six years. She morphed from a school-going girl in pigtails to a wife in charge of an entire household. As is Indian tradition, my great-grandmother handed over to her the duties and chores of taking care of and cooking for twenty-five family members on a daily basis.

Her frail build, docile and child-like face suggested a kindly, sympathetic figure, but she would often unleash a remark so wicked it would rankle all the adults of the house for some time.

My grandparents' marriage was an unfortunate one, pairing the beautiful girl from a cash-strapped family with the plain son of a clan only a touch wealthier. My grandfather's kin were largely eccentric and aloof, cast-offs from Indian society. The disparity and apparent class differences drove my great-grandmother to suicide. She ended her life at forty-three leaving behind a legacy of depression and my grandmother was left to piece together the broken shards of our family.

Monica was an unfathomable woman, and I never really understood why she did some of the things she did, like constantly needling my mother, telling her she was too dark skinned to wear bright colors or to make a suitable wife. One day, frustrated by her antics, my mother threw her plate of food on the floor dangerously close to Monica's legs.

When Monica's younger daughter, my Aunt Kaveri spent year after year attending singing lessons, why didn't grandma push her to grow and capitalize on her talent by becoming a professional? Grandmother was so deep in her depression she failed to recognize she had done a great disservice to her eldest son, my uncle by ignoring his studies and excellent grades. Why did she not acknowledge the smartness and talent of my mother, her elder daughter who should've been her companion but instead was the most reviled in the household?

Her mother's suicide dampened my grandmother's life and she often acted as though she thought of herself as bleak and insignificant. I think her mother's premature death served to harden her, making her immune to the harsh realities of life.

Monica's complexion was fair – the colour of warm milk. To brighten her skin tone even more, she layered cold cream on her face and neck, and sealed it in with talcum powder. I could smell her from afar when I returned from school – she was always engulfed in a haze of cream and talc.

I remember her thick glossy hair had, over the years, been reduced to wispy strands that she tied in a long ponytail and rolled into a bun. In later years, she added artificial hair to thicken the braid that had grown thinner and thinner with age.

Grandma was physically brittle too; her legs had been fractured on multiple occasions, thanks to her tendency to wander about the house without the aid of her trusty walking stick. She did not take good care of herself and even spooned sugar into her numerous cups of tea despite being diabetic. She always drank directly from the saucer, sipping, a sly smile creeping across her alabaster face. She never drank milk even though a string of doctors warned her to start before her bones crumbled. I cringe whenever I recall how she skipped her medicines and feasted on rice and dishes expressly forbidden by her doctor.

Despite her ill health, I am pleased she was able to meet both her sons-in-law, though she couldn't attend either my or my sister's weddings. On both occasions she was laid up in bed, the second time having broken her leg by trying to hang her own clothes and slipping on the smooth tiles of the balcony.

I do regret the fact she never met my children, her great-grandchildren, though she had plenty of opportunities to do so. I vowed to never treat my daughter the way she treated hers. I would never foist my frustrations on children too young to understand. This is easier said than done, of course and even now, I have to catch myself before unloading the frustration of a ten-hour workday onto a six-year-old for whom the world is still rosy.

Even though we were radically different, Grandmother might have been smarter than I gave her credit for. She taught me to be independent, practical and realistic yet she was neither completely traditional nor overtly feminist. She never imposed any restrictions on me and my sister, but she was very hard on my mother, her daughter. Maybe it was because my mother's skin was a shade darker than her own.

The last time I saw her, she was laying on a hospital bed, after yet another operation on her leg. As I stood by her, she whispered, "Promise me that you will come to meet me more often. And remember to take good care of your family."

I kept her second wish, and trust that she, in her heavenly abode, is happier for it.

The Girl In The Gold Dress
By Kim Bussing

I slide into her dress, twist and wiggle and contort until I can finally tug the zipper up, and I am securely fastened into the draping layers of silk and lace. The mirror assures me I am a princess. I have unearthed a pair of kitten heels from my mother's closet as well, and I twirl, convinced I am a duchess from a foreign land, a queen preparing to regale her subjects, some enchanted fairy tale figure.

My mother appears in the doorway. I see her behind me, in the mirror, and I curtsy before her. The billowing skirt of the dress sweeps outward, the gold fabric is soft, and unassumingly sensual about my legs.

My mother is a pretty woman, with hair that has gone prematurely grey. As she watches me, young and fair and innocent, she smiles but her eyes are elsewhere.

She tells me: You look just like her.

It is only because her name is so rarely invoked, because she is often mentioned in impersonal pronouns instead of more familiar terms, that I know we are talking about my grandmother. Nancy.

The first time I heard them mention my grandmother, I thought they were talking about a monster. The woman they painted was no woman at all: a recluse, hidden somewhere in the Midwest in a place with no heat, no electricity, no running water. A creature haunted by visions that led her to reject any world that wasn't a construct of her own polluted mind.

Through the fault of bad genetics, or a traumatic childhood, or God, my grandmother is schizophrenic. I have never met her. The concept of a grandmother is foreign to me, because for so many of my childhood years, the word was inherently connected with fear on my part, disgust on my father's, sheltered sorrow on my mother's.

What I know of a grandmother is one whose mental illness was passed to her children like hand-me-downs.

Her schizophrenia officially manifested when my mother was graduating high school. So in a way you can say my mother was the lucky one—she lost a parent when she was just old enough to shoulder the burden of orphanage, as my grandfather left almost as soon as my grandmother adopted her own personal brand of crazy.

To delve into the full horror of what it was like for my aunts to grow up in her household would be impossible — I am not privy to the memories; in many ways, I'm not sure my aunts are, either.

What can be said is that rules were enforced. Doors were shuttered. Curtains were drawn on windows so the house became like a tomb. My grandmother ranted about the government. She accused her husband of trying to poison her, maintained that her children were soon to be targets of the government, the neighbors, their absentee father.

The full truth of those years is buried, but the damage done at times appears irreversible. The middle daughter is now nearing fifty and living alone, isolated from friends and has never come close to marriage. The youngest turned almost madly to religion, leaving for Africa twenty years ago, where she contracted a dangerous gastrointestinal illness that forced her to return home. As though fate were forever mocking her, the antibiotics given to help her instead gave her chronic fatigue, a disease that has confined her to a small apartment for the past two decades. She cannot work and is dependent upon aid from the government as well as frequent assistance from friends, my aunt, and my grandfather.

It is possible to recover from chronic fatigue in fewer than six years. But for my aunt it is not an illness—the constant care and attention makes it the childhood she never received.

Years after the dress incident, I searched through boxes my mother had stuffed with memories and found an envelope from her sisters. It was a tape from one of my mother's birthday parties transferred to DVD, and I watched it. And then I watched it again.

I had never seen her before, my grandmother. She was a strikingly beautiful woman, slender with delicate features. Glossy dark hair. There was no sound, but how often she threw back her head in laughter assured you she was someone that drew people to her, like an exotic flower, or a crime scene.

My mother found me watching the videos and took a seat beside me on our faded green couch. We were silent, like the footage. It was a bit like watching a horror movie. You know something bad is going to happen, that some dragon is going to fell the heroine but even with your knowledge, you cannot help but deny it. It is impossible to believe that such a stunning woman could descend so thoroughly into madness.

I like to think of her wearing the gold dress. I like to think of her so young, so hopeful, twirling in front of the mirror as it assured her she was the most beautiful girl in the kingdom. I hold precious those stories about her that are told at night, as if they are secrets that should be buried—stories of her imagination, her enthusiasm, her boundless love for the world and those around her. Those are not the traits of a schizophrenic. Those are the traits of someone I recognize when I stare in the mirror, wearing my own clothes.

Psychologists have described what happened with a variety of explanations: there was physical and sexual abuse, emotional abandonment, crippling poverty, a menagerie of factors that somehow reduced her from a women dashing around in a gold dress to someone isolated, huddled in a frozen house in the Midwest with a cracked roof and glass jars filled with her own urine.

But even though we have never met, she is my grandmother. She sends me letters every year, through my mother, that I have just started to read. Despite the madness, there is a love in her for her family that is perhaps more poignant than many medically sane people possess.

Even though we have never met, she is my grandmother. Someone who suffered and was the catalyst for other's suffering, but still my grandmother. She was a stranger to me, and a forbidden topic for my mother and aunts, but still my grandmother. And I do her the only honor I can, by remembering who she used to be. I imagine her as enchanted with the world, struck by the beauty in it; someone who felt things more affectingly and fully than those around her. I imagine her as bewitching, sociable; her dark hair perfectly styled, her makeup immaculate.

I imagine her trapped in an ivory tower of her own suffering, with no one to climb up and rescue her, but still a princess, endlessly twirling in her gold gown.

Frances, You're Going to Be Just Fine
By Dawn Corrigan

I don't cook.

I toast, I boil water, I make coffee. That's it.

In the past, I microwaved, but then at a cocktail party one night, a doctor's wife told me microwaves are the Devil and cause cancer and that was the end of that.

The woman's husband was a gynecologist, so he, and for that matter, his wife, were unlikely experts on appliances as sources of physical or spiritual malaise. But I didn't care. Her words confirmed my suspicions. The next day I unplugged the microwave and drove it to Goodwill.

My avoidance of the kitchen and its appliances is puzzling. It's not like I wasn't exposed to decent cooking as a kid. Both parents were good cooks, as were a myriad of aunts and cousins, even a few uncles.

My grandmothers, however, were a different story. By all accounts, both of them—the one who died when I was five, and the one who's still alive today, albeit addled with dementia—were terrible cooks. Therefore, I suspect it's one of those traits that skips a generation.

Before she took up residence in the assisted living facility, my living grandmother was able to make merry about her handicap. She would tell her visitors, "I'm going to make you my specialty," and laughingly put on a pot of water for some Lipton tea.

I always admired Grandma's chutzpah, as well as the hint of defiance it suggested. Italian-American women are supposed to cook, and be ashamed if they can't. I suspect my Nan's refusal to get sucked into this role was a rebellion of sorts whose first guerrilla battle was waged long before I was born.

But I have to admit, I would have admired this rebellion even more if it had been tied to a larger cause. Feminism springs to mind. But beyond that, I would have been happy had I thought my Nan neglected our family's physical hungers—which, after all, were being addressed by many other members of the clan—because she was so concerned with, say, our spiritual needs.

Unfortunately, this wasn't the case. Don't get me wrong, Nan had her religion. Hers was that brand of Catholicism that involves lots of prayer cards and rosary beads and the giving of gifts that, when you open the card and read the message, turn out to be an announcement that a Mass will be said in your honor the following Sunday.

Nice in its way, but not the sort of gift that satisfies a child who's looking for Rock'em Sock'em Robots, or a stack of Nancy Drews.

Even the unsatisfactory gift giving, however, would have been all right if it appeared to provide Nan with some genuine spiritual solace. But it didn't—at least, not if you consider acceptance of mortality to be an indicator of spiritual peace.

I've never met a person more terrified of death. I was about five years old when Nan began speaking mournfully of her own evidently imminent passing, incidentally warning me that if I didn't follow her wishes to the letter I would be written right out of the will, and thus excluded from a largess that could not be long in coming.

Not until later did it occur to me that Nan was only fifty at the time of these conversations, and how weird it was for a healthy fifty-year-old woman to incessantly prophesize her own death. Reports of her death's imminence were clearly exaggerated. Decade after decade, she has endured.

Her health was another mystery. The woman got no exercise, not even the light exercise some people get performing housework, since all of the housekeeping was left to her third husband, Dom. She lived on sugar, cigarettes, *True Detective* stories, playing the slot machines, and vindictiveness. Yet she outlived her parents, two husbands, seven brothers, and both of my maternal grandparents.

Did this unexpected longevity bring her any happiness? It appeared not. She continued to tremulously announce her own slightly delayed passing at all family gatherings. Cancer was her particular obsession. However, since her own body remained stubbornly cancer-free, the relationship remained a hypothetical one until, at the age of 75, she found a dermatologist who made a tidy living removing moles from obsessive compulsives.

Thereafter, at least once every six weeks she'd announce triumphantly that the doctor had found and removed another mole and that it had indeed turned out to be cancerous. She'd describe with great relish how deeply he'd needed to dig into the skin to remove the offending blot, how large a hole remained, how strong was the pain.

Meanwhile, our other relatives were dropping like flies from lung cancer, breast cancer, AIDS. There were even some genuine skin cancer scares. Nan's exaggeration of her own health—issues seems too strong a word; let's go with inconveniences—was insensitive, to say the least. But no one pointed this out to her.

Then, my Aunt Vicky died. Aunt Vicky was everyone's favorite. A laugher, a singer, a dancer, but smart too, and sometimes sad under all the surface charm.

She used to say, "It would be easy if we were stupid. If we were stupid, we'd be happy all the time."

She wasn't even sixty when lung cancer got her.

After her funeral, I moped around my parents' house for a couple weeks. One afternoon Nan and Dom showed up. My parents were both at work, so I played hostess and let them in. Nan and I sat at the kitchen table while Dom settled in front of the TV.

"You know, Dawn," Nan said, "When I visited your Aunt Vicky in the hospital, the doctor came in. It was all 'Cancer this' and 'Cancer that.' I didn't like it."

"It's not like she didn't know she had cancer, Nan."

"I don't care. It's not right. 'Cancer, cancer, cancer'— who needs it?" Nan declared. "When I'm in the hospital dying, I don't want to hear the 'C' word! I want everyone nice and cheerful, and the doctor to sail in and say, 'Frances, you're going to be just fine!' You'll be there, making sure it's like that, won't you?"

"Sure, Nan. Where else would I be?"

Departures
By Melanie Bryant

Standing at the kitchen sink looking out of the window, I caught my first glimpse of the damage the California sun had done to the garden. The pink geraniums were lanky; their flowers burned a deep fuchsia from the unrelenting sun. The roses, too, had seen better days, their petals wilted and curled from the heat. Even the tomatoes seemed tired, as if they were waiting for cooler weather to get back to business. Earlier in the week, I had picked the last of the peaches from the tree and lined them up across the windowsill where I could admire them.

I was going to make a peach cobbler, although, I had no idea why—I didn't even like peach cobbler—but at some point over the course of the week, after numerous admiring glances at their blushing beauty, I decided that it would be the last grand gesture of summer. So, in spite of the heat, I went to work on the cobbler, peeling and slicing the peaches and mixing the spices and flour. I hadn't been thinking about much of anything as I worked, but the intricate way memory is woven into our taste buds must have stirred something deep within me. I hadn't been able to resist the peaches and when I took my first bite, it took me back to another August, some 36 years earlier. It was the taste of those peaches that made me think about my maternal grandmother, Sophie. At first, my thoughts were concrete: the color of her hair, the clothes she wore, the way she missed my grandfather after his death and never remarried. But, memory is complex and soon my thoughts turned to other matters: the complexity of our relationship, my distant and cool attitude toward her, because after my grandfather died, she never could move on. No matter what I did to persuade her otherwise, she loved me unconditionally.

Growing up, my brother and I spent a lot of time at our grandparents' house, especially after my father left. It had been expected; my father was charismatic and handsome with a penchant for keeping secrets. Clearly, he had not been cut out for marriage and a family.

In remaking her life, my mother developed a certain edge; she wore more fashionable clothes and enrolled at the local community college where she studied Native American history. On occasion, we would catch her smoking cigarettes. She joined one of those newly formed and much needed social groups of the mid 1970s for people who found themselves suddenly single. On Fridays, there was Beyond Divorce and on Saturdays, Parents without Partners. Sometimes she would go out both nights, but eventually, while both groups had their merits, she whittled it down to one or the other. The nights my mother went out were the nights we spent with my grandparents.

Sundays at Grandma Sophie and Bop's house were family days. My grandparents served dinner at noon sharp and everyone was expected to be at the table, including my uncle and aunt and younger cousin who were living with my grandparents at the time. After dessert and dishes, we'd clean ourselves up and pile into my grandfather's big brown sedan, and with my grandfather at the helm, a half chewed cigar between his teeth, we'd pull off into the afternoon. Sometimes we'd drive up to the mountains, maybe Pike's Peak, other times we'd go to the mall and window shop. Sometimes we would tour the new model homes they were building a few towns over. We never went very far. At five, we'd be back around the kitchen table, heating up leftovers and eating our supper.

One day, my grandmother convinced my grandfather to take us on an overnight trip to Grand Junction so we could pick peaches. This was an exciting prospect and I couldn't wait to go. It meant we would be eating at a restaurant, and perhaps my grandfather would pay extra and we'd stay at a motel with a swimming pool. I was ten years old and traveled everywhere with a worn out stuffed cow, named Cow Moo Moo.

****

The motel was old and worn, the room twice as big as usual to accommodate the extra beds and a couch. There was no swimming pool. I felt uneasy, so despite her awful smelling cold cream, I begged my grandmother to sleep with me. I dozed off in my place against the wall, Cow Moo Moo tucked safely in my arms, and me, tucked safely into my grandmother's.

The next morning, we were up early and off to the orchard. We packed before leaving the motel and loaded our bags into the car; after a morning in the orchard, we'd be back on the road. I didn't realize it at the time, but in our haste to get to the peach orchard, I had forgotten Cow Moo Moo between the wall and the mattress where he'd quietly slipped from my grasp during the night.

My mother was the last to leave the room and when she finally emerged, she was dressed in a matching blue jean outfit with rhinestone roses on the jacket. She slid into the car beside me and my grandfather started the engine, slowly making his way to the main road.

By the time we climbed up the ladders in the orchard, the sun was already cresting the hills, the dew in the branches sparkling like hundreds of tiny diamonds. We set to work, picking fat peaches and loading them into our buckets. I was the fastest picker until I reached out and plucked a spider along with a peach. I screamed and the ladder shook beneath my weight as I quickly and clumsily dropped to the ground, the bucket of peaches spilling out around me. Although my mother calmly explained to me that spiders lived in peach trees and yes, peaches were furry, but they were not covered in hair, I refused to pick anymore peaches and after a flurry of tears, it was decided that we should begin the long drive back home.

My grandfather was making good time on the highway when I realized that Cow Moo Moo was gone. I had left him behind in the old motel room, pasted between the wall and the squeaky bed. My heart sank and I screamed in panic.

My grandfather was adamant that we continue; it was too far to go back. But over my tears and pleadings, I could hear the steady, calm voice of my grandmother as she insisted he turn the car around. The car grew quiet and my grandparents entered into a silent standoff; my grandfather continued down the highway, my grandmother locked eyes with him in the rear view mirror. After the second highway marker, my grandfather gave up his silence for a burst of cursing and exited the highway to begin the trek back to the motel to retrieve my Cow Moo Moo.

Soon after that trip, my mother met my stepfather at one of her social events and they got married. Our overnight trips to visit our grandparents became less frequent. We moved into a new neighborhood, into a new house, and the distance between our home and that of my grandparents grew considerably.

I was fourteen when my grandfather died after a heart attack.

Once I got over the grief of losing him, I wanted my grandmother to date and maybe, remarry. I was a dreamy romantic who thought only of boys and love. My friend, Barbie, whose grandmother had also been recently widowed, also fueled my desire. Unlike my own grandmother, Barbie's grandmother wore fashionable clothes, sleek leather boots with tasseled zippers, make up and perfume. She took up dancing and had caught the eye of a widower, on the mend himself. Together, they took up traveling to exotic locales. Barbie's grandmother sent post cards, pictures of lush and foreign scenery and brought back souvenirs, and when the widower, who was several years older, suffered a stroke and had to be moved into a home, Barbie's grandmother quickly found another suitor and moved on.

Instead of traveling to exotic locales, my grandmother took the bus to the cemetery and tended my grandfather's grave, a trip she'd make twice a week for the next 29 years until her heart finally gave out, too.

Over the last decades of our relationship, I had become distant and cool; disinterested. I was living in California, married, and climbing the career ladder. I still sent cards for special occasions and I made an effort to call once or twice a year, but I only saw her once in the year or two before I had moved away to California. The last ten years of her life, I didn't see her at all. Still, she didn't love me any less, she never missed a beat with her letters or gifts—she was still as generous and as thoughtful as ever.

I don't know if it was the taste of the peaches that made me think about love, or if it was the memory of my grandmother. I do know that I learned about love that day. The twists and turns of fate had lessened my cool reserve that had seemed so chic in my twenties. I understood love was the hard road, the obstacles and ruts, the parts where you had to turn back to where you'd already been because it was important to someone else. Love was taking the worst that someone gave you and overlooking it. Love was holding on to those you loved, even after they had long been gone.

She Taught Me Unconditional Love
By Cathy Thomason

As children, it is important to have someone in our lives who loves us unconditionally. My father's mother was that person in my life. Granny, as I called her, introduced me to embroidery, Italian dressing, the public library and some teachings, including the importance of unconditional love, that have stayed with me throughout my life.

My grandfather died at an early age, leaving Granny with seven children, ages one to twenty-one. Granny's only income was from the sewing she did for others and that was supplemented from the earnings of the older children. In Granny's later years, she lived with her children and their families on a rotating basis, particularly when her health began to fail.

I loved having Granny stay with us on the farm outside the small northern Alabama town where I grew up in the 50s and 60s. She let me play dress-up in her Sunday hats, gloves, purses, and glittering pins, and always had time for my never-ending, childish questions. Granny's patience seemed infinite in any given situation and I'm sure I tried her patience often, although she never let on.

Granny thought all females should learn needlework as she was very accomplished at this herself. The summer of 1958 when I was eight years old, Granny decided to teach my sister and me how to embroider. She gave us each a scarf stamped with a simple flower design. We selected the flosses in the colors we liked and she proceeded to give us instructions. We were to work on the scarves at an appointed time each day until they were complete. My sister has always been one of the most organized individuals I know. When we finished doing the needlework for the day, her scarf was neatly folded and put away in a drawer. Alas, mine was balled up, tossed onto the floor of the closet, and usually had to be dug out from underneath whatever had landed on top of it during the course of the day.

My sister made perfectly precise embroidery stitches. Mine were uneven and consisted mainly of tangled knots. Granny just smiled her sweet smile while she sat patiently and helped me snip the tangled threads, all the while talking quietly to an increasingly restless eight-year-old. My sister completed her scarf and it was as pristine as the day she began. My scarf was never finished and was grimy to boot. Embroidery was for me an exercise in frustration. Yet, Granny's smile never wavered, nor did she ever utter words that would have been hurtful.

Granny had fourteen grandchildren and never forgot a birthday. You knew you would get a birthday card from Granny no matter where she might be when your birthday rolled around. You also knew that inside the card would be a sweet handwritten note and, if you were a girl, a beautiful snow white handkerchief with lovely embroidery. A young lady should never be without a handkerchief. This was one of Granny's teachings as was the one that a thank-you note should immediately be written for any present received. I still never leave home without a supply of Kleenex and penned handwritten thank-you notes, even in this day of social media.

Granny had a favorite saying, one I heard a lot and by no means a favorite of mine as it was directed at me too often. I did hear it spoken with regards to others from time to time, but in a gentle, loving voice. I always felt I wasn't an attractive child and would sometimes fish for a compliment from Granny. I would look in the mirror, sigh loudly, and proclaim, "I wish I was pretty!"

Granny's stock reply was, "Pretty is as pretty does."

One day, when I was five, while exploring our attic, Granny, my sister and I discovered three Nancy Drew mysteries that had belonged to my older sister. Granny decided that my sister and I needed to spend more time with books. Each night before bedtime, Granny would read aloud a chapter from one of the books. Granny found she had a spellbound audience in my sister and me. Soon, she decided it was time to introduce us to the public library. She had Dad drive us into town and in a small two-roomed library a whole new world opened up to us. My sister and I devoured everything in the library although mysteries were our favorite genre. Even now, seldom do I enter a library anywhere in the world and not think of climbing a flight of stairs hand in hand with Granny to arrive at what was for me one of the happiest places on earth. Granny didn't live long enough to witness how her encouraging our literary pursuits resulted in my having a thirty-five-year career as a librarian. She would have been very proud.

Granny didn't cook a lot when she was with us but she did have a cake recipe that I have treasured over the years. Her chocolate pound cake, made with plain old Hershey's cocoa, was to die for. It was like velvet on the tongue with heady scents of creamy butter and vanilla.

As for that Italian salad dressing, who would have thought that her finely shredded iceberg lettuce, enough black pepper to provoke a hearty sneeze, and Wishbone could rival any salad made by our famous chefs of today? I think it was the love that went into its making that made it so special.

Granny's death in 1963 was a very difficult time for me. I lost someone who loved me unconditionally and taught me the meaning of unconditional love. I know this and the many other things I learned from Granny are a part of who I am. I am thankful for all that she taught me, even the dreaded, "Pretty is as pretty does."

Grandma Gave Us Roots and Wings
By Joan Gary

Whenever I smell lavender, I think of grandma. And, for a brief moment, I become a child again.

I was just five when I had to live with grandma. I still recall how much I cried when my mother left me and how grandma tried, so tenderly, to explain this wasn't forever. She told me mother would return for visits, send me letters, and take me home in a few months.

I remember mother's letters. As soon as they arrived, grandma would give them to me. I would look up at her and say, "grandma, read my letter, you know I can't read." She would smile and sit down, still wearing her kitchen apron. I'd sit on the floor, close to her, hanging on her every word. After she read my letter, I'd put it in my dress pocket.

I especially remember the times when my grandma smiled because she didn't smile very often. But when she did, it was like the sun rising and setting all at the same time.

The time came when I did return home; the first few months were especially hard for my mother. Everything she did, I complained about. She would cook and I would say, "Why don't you use a cookbook, like grandma does?" Or, she would cook my favorite West Indian dumplings and I would whine, "Grandma doesn't cook dumplings like THAT!" Although I was glad to be home, I missed my grandma and her overcrowded little house in the south of England. It was overcrowded because my uncle, aunt and her children lived there too!

Grandchildren were constantly running around, shouting and laughing and doing the mischievous things kids usually do. My grandma never complained.

Owning a home in 1960 England wasn't unusual, but being black and owning a home was practically unheard of. Immigrants from the West Indies usually rented rooms in other people's homes. My grandma wanted a better life for her family so her first goal was to save as much as she could to buy her own home.

Grandma gave her children all the opportunities she never had as she came from a poor farming family. So, her children were educated, had families and lived in their own homes. Yet my grandma was never really happy in England. Perhaps that's why she rarely smiled.

I was in my 30s when grandma became very ill after a series of strokes. The strokes took away her ability to walk unassisted and later she developed diabetes and eventually went blind. Finally, another stroke took away her speech. We were devastated. She tried so hard to recover after each medical blow, but suffered so much in the process.

After the last stroke, there was a call from the hospital telling us that she was slipping away. We drove like bats out of hell to get to her. But she took her last breath without us. We wanted to be there, around her, to hold her hands as she left this world but that didn't happen.

I'm old now, but the child that I was, and the woman I became, still misses and loves her grandma.

Grandma's Obituary
By Cortney Stewart

Patsy Ann Blair (née Burton), age 63, of Elizabethtown, Kentucky passed away quietly, surrounded by family at Hardin Memorial Hospital after her respirator was removed and her lungs stopped pumping much needed oxygen through her cancer-saturated body. *I don't need some goddamn doctor's machine keeping me alive.* She died on Wednesday, August 5th, 2009, days after she was rushed to the hospital, unconscious and unresponsive while her children and grandchildren shed panicked tears in the waiting room. A hospital chaplain stood unwanted in the corner until he offered to go fetch coffee. *He might as well get up off his ass, none of us wanted him here.*

She was born on September 22, 1945, one of five children, the oldest girl. She was the owner of the former Dixie House Restaurant in Clarkson, Kentucky where she drank too many cups of strong hot coffee and chain-smoked cigarettes in the corner booth, wearing a striped, short-sleeved, button down shirt with a pocket above her breast for the latest pack of cigarettes. *And y'all better not leave me without any damn smokes. Send em with me when you put me in my box—a cheap one, don't you go spending all my money on that.* She left her oldest daughter to manage most of the day-to-day business and spent Sundays in the office delivering sermons on how things ought to be done in her restaurant. *Ain't anybody going to say my restaurant is dirty.* Before that she drove a semi-truck all over the country and before that she was a no-nonsense school bus driver and before all that she was a mother taking care of her children between would-be male providers. *The bunch of goddamn idiots, at least none of them was Republicans.*

Survivors include her third husband, Robert Blair, whom she married at the Hardin County Court House. *Just me and the family, none of that who's-got-more-money shit, sealed with sterling silver rings. No sense in spending too much on them, but Rob wanted to do something, the fool man. It was followed by a party at home, where everyone was so happy that no one cared how much cake the kids were eating.* And three daughters, Alma Jean, Patty Jean, and Gina; two sons, Bobby and Mike; and a brother, Evert. Also surviving are 14 grandchildren; and nine great-grandchildren.

She was preceded in death by her beloved parents, William Wesley and Alma Alice; her ex-husband and long time friend, Jim; two sons, Jerry Lee, her oldest, who she had at age 16. *He had an accident at work on a river barge. Someone pushed him, I just know it. My Jerry was too sharp for an accident like that,* and Johnny Wayne. *Who died in a hit-and-run at age 16. Goddamn drunk drivers—a mama should never have to bury her babies;* her baby sister, Darlene; and two brothers, Tommy, who died alone in a nursing home in Florida, and Charlie, *Evert's twin who scared all of the kids with his throat-cancer robot voice.*

Funeral services will be conducted at 2:00 pm Saturday, August 8, 2009, in the chapel of Dixon-Atwood & Trowbridge Funeral Home, *unlike all of the previous family funerals, which were held at the Brown Funeral Home. Patty and Alma said they're gonna need more room with so many people. Brown's been going downhill anyway. Jim's funeral wasn't nearly as nice as Jerry's.* Rev. Kyle Page will officiate. *He's from Alma's church. He's not bad for a pastor, even if they are all a bunch of damn hypocrites.*

Burial will follow in Mt. Zion Cemetery across from her in-laws. *They're gonna be much better company than all those crazy-ass Burtons in the Elizabethtown Memorial Gardens.* A Baptist meal will follow at Mt. Zion, *in celebration of an old lady who, between cups of coffee and chain smoking, was always making sure that people got fed. They'd better have plenty of coffee too, my girls are gonna need it. It will be more like a family reunion than a wake, although tissues will still be provided. Shut up with all that crying, I'm not gone forever—I'll be up there waitin.*

Visitation will be Thursday from 4:00-8:00 pm, Friday 10:00 am-8:00 pm, and Saturday after 9 am, and *it will be filled with most of the population of Clarkson who loved the old lady despite her heathen, chain-smoking ways.*

Planting Seeds
By Jody E. Lebel

On my window ledge sits a yellow plastic cup with a tiny zinnia seedling pushing up over the rim, a school project for my granddaughter, Kayla. The cup is graced with a picture of the adult flower she cut out of a magazine and pasted on the front. Memories of visits to my grandma's bring a smile as I help her little hands tend to her plant, moving it from room to room to catch the perfect light.

My grandmother Margaret, loved to plant seeds. Morning glories, raised from seeds, climbed high every summer. I remember holding the ladder while she pounded nails up into the eaves to hold the twine for the plants to twist around. Many warm afternoons were spent playing paper dolls on her porch behind the flowered privacy wall. As soon as the ground was ready, Grandma planted her little garden out back in the sunny part of her small property. She raised radishes, carrots and tomatoes. In my mind I can still picture the green sprouts peeking out of neat rows. At the end of each row stood a wooden stake with the seed packet carefully tied to it. She had four brown mounds along the back where fat cucumbers grew.

Grandma Margaret especially loved to plant gift seeds. Gift seeds to her were the ones you get when you open a fresh orange or a peach. Her windowsills were filled with jelly jars of backyard dirt and little seedlings of lemon and apple trees. You didn't buy soil in packages back then. It was just the crumbly earth from her back yard. She had a sweet potato and an avocado. There was a pineapple plant and a cherry tree. They flourished all winter in her sunny porch windows.

One fall day while walking back from the corner store she spotted an acorn that had sprouted. Her face lit up and she carefully gathered it up out of the ground and took it home. She planted it in a pickle jar where it was happy until it grew out of space so she transferred it into a paint can, then a bucket, then a rain barrel. When it was obvious it had to go into the ground she brought it to my mother's house, where there was over an acre of land, and lovingly planted it in the back yard. Every year we would take Grandma's picture standing by it, then under it. The tree thrived and when my mom sold her property we worried that the new owners might not like a huge oak tree by the house, but it was still standing the day we moved out of state. At that point it had been 35 years since Grandma brought it home.

I dug out a photo of Grandma Margaret to show to Kayla. Some day we're going to plan a car trip and see if Grandma's oak tree is still there. In the meantime, the wonder of watching things grow has passed down to another generation. Thanks Grandma.

Never Really Gone
By Krysten Lindsay Hager

Today marks twenty-two years since my Grandma Lillian passed away. On one hand, I can't believe she's been gone this long. I sometimes forget just how young I was when she left us. However, part of the reason I can't believe her passing was so long ago is because my family still feels her presence so strongly. I wish I could say I see her in a sunset or hear her in a newborn baby's cry—something poetic, but nope. That's not it at all. I see her hand in my life when my water heater dies on a day my house is a mess and I have to clean it to let in a repair person. I hear her when I reach for a new magazine and I overhear fellow shoppers saying, "You and those crazy celebrity tabloids. Do you need that? Save your money," and I look around to see if they're speaking to me. Or any time I find myself thinking some athlete or actor is cute, only to find out he's Polish or Russian. I swear, that woman knew every Polish actor on the planet and if their name came up or their face appeared on TV, the first words out of her mouth were, "By the way, he's Polish." I now catch myself doing it.

I remember the way she would never let me buy any music or product from any celebrity who was found to be either abusive or had cheated on their spouse. I'll never forget the day this one singer appeared in a commercial. I thought he was so good looking and told my grandmother I wanted to buy one of his CDs. She didn't sugarcoat it. She detailed his abusive history with his ex-wife and made it known it was unacceptable to listen to his music. (How she knew these things, I will never know, because she certainly didn't read the tabloids). She used to say it wasn't about judgement, it was about not allowing standards to slide where we accept women being treated badly.

I see her hand in the little things and I have also felt her in the big moments in my life as well. I know she was with me in spirit when I graduated from high school and later from college. Sometimes I hear a song that reminds me of her on the radio at the exact moment I need her most. I heard the song, "Wind Beneath My Wings," which we played at her funeral, right before I got out of the car to attend my college graduation. On bad days, I often see lilies of the valley or a yellow rose—two of her favorites types of flowers.

My mother jokingly calls me "Lily," because shortly after Grandma died, everyone began to notice how much I took after her. It started when we found pictures of her when she was a young woman and she posed the same way I do. It was eerie to see how often she put her hand up by her throat, something I do all the time. None of us had ever noticed her doing it before.

Odder yet was finding a picture of her when she was in her 20s wearing a dress almost identical to something I own today. It makes me smile when I realize how much of her style has influenced me. After all, she was the one who bought me books on makeup so I'd know how to apply it properly. She used to tell me I used too much on my skin and how all those chemicals in the moisturizers and foundations were bad for me.

It wasn't until I ended up living on an island and ran out of all my cleansers, creams and serums, and was left with only a bar of soap that I finally caught on. Within a week of using just soap, my skin was flawless. Did I ever feel stupid after all those years of spending money on fancy products when a three-dollar bar of soap would have changed my skin. Lesson learned, Grandma.

She was further vindicated when all the studies about unsafe chemicals in moisturizers and sunscreens and the importance of vitamin D from the sun came out. What do I use to moisturize now? Coconut oil found in my pantry... just like she did years ago.

I even hear her voice in the way I speak. I've been known to slap my hand over my mouth when I hear one of her direct quotes slip out.

"That's not even me, that's Grandma talking," I'll say in amazement.

I also inherited her sense of humor. For instance, I find myself almost falling off the couch laughing while watching TV. Sometimes I even watch her old favorites that we used to watch together like, "The Mary Tyler Moore Show" or Carole Lombard movies. It feels like the old days when we'd watch TV together—her in her favorite chair and me in my small rocking chair, with both of us balancing a bowl of air puffed popcorn on our knees.

I find comfort in eating the foods she made best. I am connected to her whenever I make and eat chicken soup. She would be happy to know after years of getting after me, I will finally eat the cooked celery in the soup. She would also be happy to learn that instead of looking to synthetic supplements, I now try to get my vitamins from Whole Foods like she tried to tell me as a teen.

I have felt she was watching over me each time a situation would present itself and, through some odd turn of events, something would lead me away from what could have been a disaster. What seemed like a missed opportunity at the time would always later be revealed to have been a, "crisis averted." There was never any looking back wondering, "what could have been," or, "if only," because the truth somehow managed to find its way out. I knew it wasn't just luck, but that was someone looking out for me. She made sure I wasn't going to throw my life away on something fleeting.

She had always been particularly vigilant when it came to boys. During my freshman year of college, I asked for a sign about a guy I was considering dating. Within twenty-four hours, he shared a short story with me he had written that made it clear he was not right for me. I thought the one sign was a fluke, but I cannot tell you how many times something intervened when it came to me making a decision about a guy. My mom would say, "Oh that's Lillian right there." There was never any denying it. There was further proof when a box of her crystal (which had been missing for over a decade) mysteriously showed up the night before my bridal shower.

My mother said, "Grandma managed to get you a gift."

The box contained the crystal candlesticks, champagne glasses, and sugar and creamer set she had received for her own bridal shower.

Grandma may be gone physically, but she lives on when I use her recipes and in the stories about her that I've shared with others and have published. I admit her common sense wasn't always welcome to me when I was a young teen. After all, I'm a dreamer and a bit of a romantic, but as I grew up (and wised up) I realized she had been a romantic, too. She just kept her common sense in check.

I wish she could be around to talk to and call directly for advice, but she makes her presence known so I thank her for being one of my guardian angels now.

Virgo Rising
By Lesley Sheridan

Two fellow Virgos peeled potatoes together in a tiny 1980s kitchen; one steadied a knife of dense metal, and the other struggled with flimsy plastic. Grandmother and granddaughter stood quietly on both sides of a dampened mass of discarded, leathery potato skins, staring out the window and sharing quick smiles.

I'm not sure that my kitchen abilities have grown considerably since my plastic cutlery beginnings, possibly because of my reliance on processed convenience food, and partly due to the loss of a skilled teacher. At the ripe age of 31, I'm more of a microwave girl than a laborer of pots and pans. I do maintain an affinity for carbohydrates, and luckily potatoes fare just fine in microwave environments.

To describe my father's mother in one word would prove daunting, as she seems to own so many adjectives thrown about by her offspring at family get-togethers. Perhaps the simplest description lies in the antonyms, the words never used to describe a woman I wish I'd known longer—a woman never known as timid.

Images of her youth show a stunning prettiness of German heritage: sharp cheekbones, glossy raven hair that I would only see as a pepper and salt mixture, and the complexion of a China doll—a rich contrast against her inky hair in yellowed black and white photography. She carried herself well, dainty wrists folded against her torso and eyes with the focus of an owl—a bold and fearless expression.

I doubt I can ever accomplish my grandmother's seamless blend of femininity and feminism. In today's world of financially strapped double-income families, omnipresent technology and equal work expectations of women without the decency of equal pay, I wonder at times how much progress we've really made.

In her modest 65 years of life, Kathryn Eitel Johnson birthed nine children, buried two and raised a family nourished on tough times and perseverance. Together, they never missed a Sunday in church. She sustained a marriage to one man and followed the vows of "til death do us part" while maintaining a home built on the values of compassion, empathy, and honesty. Her closet stayed meek with essentials: a dress, a pair of slacks, a blouse or two. And when food was scarce, her children ate blackberries every day during the lean summer months.

She welcomed motherhood as a job not taken lightly. When two police officers arrived at her home one day, under the mistaken assumption that her son (my father) had stolen a truck battery, a slight but compact five-foot-four-inch warrior rose up with common sense and a dose of literal mother wit. In a clear and steady voice, she informed the officers that six-year-olds can't lift truck batteries and that poverty doesn't prove criminality. The cops sheepishly exited the poor side of town, hopefully with more of an education than a lesson in embarrassment.

When she disagreed with someone, she never hesitated to say so and, according to my father, even had a distinct tendency to bypass mad and go "straight to crazy." Her grown sons even struggled once to hold her back from fighting a neighbor lady who simply said the wrong thing at the wrong time. I always loved that story... her reaction seems so passionate, honest, and effortlessly brave. I'm sure the neighbor lady had a different viewpoint on the matter, but I'd also venture to guess that she had it coming.

I am the exact same height as my grandmother, but I'm far from a warrior. I have my hands full with three feline "children," and I lack a basic culinary skill set. My closet is overflowing with clearance impulse buys, and my voice often disappears during staff meeting deliberations. Nearly all of my opinions sink in gray uncertainty, and I've yet to wrestle a neighbor.

I consciously avoid upsetting people, even to the detriment of my own inner calm, and I tend to turn my temper on those who love me most rather than those who fueled my rage. That temper may serve as the closest trait I have to my grandmother despite our differing targets.

Today's magazines might praise my nine to five efforts and encourage more wardrobe splurges, but what advice would my grandmother offer? Is a life of financial security a fair trade-off for the lost role of parenthood? Is a muted voice a sign of restraint or insecurity? Should a woman ever throw a punch at a loud-mouthed neighbor rather than simply quip, "Bless her heart"?

I ask the latter in jest—at least for the most part—but I have to question what my grandmother would think now of the grandchild she armed with the plastic knife. Would she approve of my absent homemaking? Would she find my shortcomings troublesome, or would she have some quick solution learned through the trials of her time?

I will never hear her answers to these questions. Maybe she previewed my fragility long ago and was disheartened to have a flaxen-haired, timid daydreamer with a shoddy knife as her kitchen assistant.

Or maybe she simply recognized that a person has to struggle through the dullness of those plastic grooves before developing the ability to rise to the occasion and handle the real thing like a pro.

Grandma's Kitchen
By Marilyn Morgan

Shades of pale and faded yellow everywhere. On the walls. On the tall wooden cabinets with bottom drawers, the kind of drawers that never fit quite right and sometimes you had to tug and tug and give them a good swift fist slam to open. On the old wooden table and chairs, their seats hollowed from years of wear. Dishes were piled a mile high in the sink, an oven door squeaked as it opened and closed, a refrigerator hummed in the corner and a screen door banged shut as a neighbor entered. This was Grandma's kitchen and this is the only place I ever remember my Grandma. It was as if she too were shades of pale yellow and a permanent fixture in her kitchen.

As a young girl when I banged through the screen door, there were never outstretched arms to greet me. No, but there was Grandma, bent over the oven, lifting out raisin-eyed sugar cookies or a tray of homemade rolls or poking donuts bubbling in hot grease. "Here, Min," she'd say scooping a cookie from the cooling tin.

Grandma was short and slightly plump. She always wore a bib apron tied securely over a faded housedress. A source of my childish fascination was her long grey braid that snaked down her back to her waist, growing slimmer and slimmer until the end was only a few strands of hair. Sometimes, the braid was wound round and round at the back of her head and stabbed with a cluster of bobby pins. Her skin was wrinkly with various sizes and shapes of black/brown moles, warts or growths, and her clear, sea blue eyes darted about keeping watch over whatever was simmering on the stove or baking in the oven.

Grandma's kitchen was a source of mouth-watering aromas, mystery and fascination. It was a gathering place for a menagerie of old women, most in some degree of infirmity. The chairs were always occupied, the teakettle always whistling on the stove, and the walls alive with chatter. There was no appointed time for arrival, but neighboring women came one by one, at any hour all day long. It wasn't at all unusual for a neighbor to visit in the morning for a while, then leave only to return in the afternoon.

Frequently, I hung on the outskirts of this scene, gobbling my sugar cookie and waiting for my cousins to arrive so we could play. The squeak of the screen door signaled a visitor.

"Hi Mable," Grandma's voice was warm and happy. "The teakettle's on."

Mable limped slowly over to the table and sat down. Not far behind was Lois, whose back boasted a very large round hump. I could not keep my eyes off the basketball size protrusion on her back. Later outside in Grandma's yard, I'd bend way over and try to walk like Lois, my body swaying back and forth like an elephant. After Lois came Mary, followed by Helen, Louise, and sometimes Betty. It was a dizzying array of women, their canes tapping across the linoleum, entering and leaving, and always there was talk.

In the way that children intuitively know that they are not supposed to hear certain adult talk, I, too, knew I was not supposed to hear and understand the crippled tales. But how fascinating this world of women became as I hovered in the corner secretly listening.

"Did you know," Lois said, "that Mary Jones was caught in the hayloft with Sam Brisson?"

I watched as hands flew to mouths muffling the guffaws.

"What about Douglas?" Betty asked. "Rheumatism so bad he can't hoe his garden anymore."

"Did you hear about Elsie?" interrupted Helen. "Sits in her room all day with the shades drawn, turning day into night"

"I didn't see Nancy in church on Sunday," said Lois.

And always the talk would find its way to Mrs. Roberts and that terrible, dirty band of foster children who lived down the road.

"Wild and crude… " The faces at the table glanced sideways at me as Grandma poured another cup of tea and said in a hushed voice, "Min is forbidden to go down there."

At that, my insides curled into a tight ball as I thought about the many times I snuck to Mrs. Roberts' to join her band of children for a raucous game of hide-and-seek or tag or even who could fart the loudest. Even as a child, I knew the world was a place of inconsistency and filled with contradiction.

I longed for a Grandma who would read me a bedtime story, tuck me in at night, pull the blanket up to my chin and sing me a lullaby. A Grandma who packed a picnic for a special walk, in the field where flowers bloomed in summer. And a Grandma who would throw her arms tight around me when I walked through the door, making me feel as if I were the most important girl in the world.

Perhaps, my Grandmother had another role to play. Betty Friedan's *The Feminine Mystique* wasn't born yet and the word feminism was largely unspoken. But Grandma offered something special to women—a place of refuge for wise, elderly, disabled souls. A place in which women felt safe and comfortable in the company of others, a way station on the long road to the twenty-first century and beyond.

Grandma Known, Unknown
By Savannah Hendricks

Every time I make apple crisp I think of Grandma Marie. Whenever I see a crossword puzzle, or find a wrinkled up Kleenex shoved into a pocket, I think of Grandma Marie. Yet, what I knew about my grandma was so little it barely skimmed the surface of her life. She was strong; spoke few words, presented independence, and had a graceful aura.

Grandma Marie dressed for herself and no one else. She wore plaid pants, pressed white button up blouses, and cream-colored sweaters. The pockets of her sweaters held reused Kleenex and hard candy. Her small frame must have hovered around one hundred pounds, and her curly hair was as white as marshmallows.

I'm not sure what most grandmas do with their grandchildren, but I am confident all grandmas have their own special ways. For instance, I cannot recall a time when Grandma Marie and I shared a hug. Was hugging not a grandma requirement? While it's possible when I was very young I might have received a hug, I am unable to relive any memories of one. I knew I was not a bad granddaughter to have caused this lack of affection. I had zero memories of Grandma Marie commenting on any of my behaviors, or questioning anything I did in her presence. Either way, she always sent me a check for my birthday and Christmas; until the year Grandpa Leo started feeding Cheetos to the birds. Things changed shortly thereafter due to Grandpa Leo's Alzheimer's disease. Airplane trips to visit Grandma Marie and Grandpa Leo stopped. Holiday cards with Grandma Marie's cursive inside lessened into a complete disappearance.

When Grandma Marie passed I did not attend her funeral. In fact, I had not seen her for many years; so many, that I do not have a memory of the actual time when I had seen her last. The final story I heard was she had been on an M&M diet of sorts.

I have memories of watching Grandma Marie cutting up apples for the crisp, and making the crumble topping for the pflaumenkuchen dessert. During my visits, Grandma Marie always made sure supper was at the same time every evening; you could count the ticks of the cuckoo clock on it.

I do remember how Grandma Marie was always on my side. She even allowed me to do things that upset Grandpa Leo and my father. Like when she overruled Grandpa Leo to let me eat my tortilla chips with melted cheese in the living room so I could cheer for the Minnesota Twins on television. She even gave me the tabloid magazines when she finished the crossword puzzles in them, against my father's protest.

Then one evening during the heat of the summer I was not able to sleep, and felt rather homesick as I lay in bed. I got up, stepped around the bugs populating the guest bedroom floor, and went out into the living room. I found Grandma Marie concentrating on her latest crossword puzzle, and told her what was wrong. Against Grandpa Leo's protests, Grandma Marie wheeled a small television into the room. I crawled back into bed, and lay there as the sounds and flickering of the television lulled me to sleep. That was the moment I knew Grandma Marie loved me, even without words.

When I think of Grandma Marie, I think of the lake cabin and Quaker Oat cereal she kept in the pantry. I think of her apple crisp made on the long counter at the house in town. I think of her leftover, flat soda pop she saved for later in the avocado green refrigerator. I think of the way she walked without a sound and would sit for hours in her living room chair, crossword puzzle in hand. I think of the night she rescued me from being homesick.

Today, her tiny, thin book, *The Child's Bible History*, sits on my bookcase. I am careful when I dust it. I have opened it a few times, finding the cursive writing of Grandma Marie's name with a date of February 10, 1929 under it. When I close the book, and return it to the shelf, I think about the grandma I didn't really know, and the few memories that will have to be enough.

Globetrotting Grandma
By Julie Brown

Grandma was conspicuous by her absence. Exotic picture postcards from Ankara, Beirut, Gibraltar, Tehran, Istanbul, Ephesus, Tripoli, Pompeii, would magically appear in my mailbox, accompanied by intriguing trinkets like a small wooden camel, a tiny, elegantly inlaid box, and a ferocious-looking stuffed monkey. These toys and postcards were most of what I knew of Grandma for the first ten years of my life. As a very young child I thought that this was normal, and that all grandparents traveled the world sending back small gifts and letters as compensation for their absence in their families' lives.

I grew up in a quiet, conservative, all-white 1950s suburb in California, where all the dads worked in offices and all the moms stayed home and baked. Our life there was routine and pleasant. It's almost impossible for today's children to imagine how isolated and narrow our lives were then. There was no one in my neighborhood that didn't look and talk exactly like me. In my insulated little life, where television had only a few flickering channels, before Internet, before computers even, my globetrotting grandparents were definitely an anomaly, and sometimes an embarrassment to me just because they were so different. Once, when Grandma came home for her yearly visit, I hid under the bed, frightened of this formidable woman who was so clearly disappointed in the shy, dreamy child who was dragged out and dusted off to say hello to her.

Grandma was a mighty force to be reckoned with! She was as round as she was tall, with expressive brown eyes, and she looked as though she should be a jolly storybook sort of grandma who kept caramels in her apron pocket for her adoring grandchildren. But Grandma always had a critical look on her face (at least when she looked at me). Her sharp, intelligent eyes could bore right through a child's brain and uncover whatever secret and silly thoughts were hiding there. In her overwhelming presence, I became tongue-tied and painfully aware of all my many shortcomings.

Grandma was born in 1907 and grew up in a small town. She married Grandpa, a welder, at age eighteen. I think that Grandpa, an easygoing and sweet man, probably could have been perfectly happy the rest of his life living quietly as a welder in that small town, but Grandma definitely had other ideas.

After raising her children, she nudged Grandpa into entering college at the same time that their son (my father) was attending. I'm sure that my father was just thrilled about going to college with his dad. Back then there were no middle-aged people in college, they would have stuck out like sore thumbs. I'm not sure how Grandma got them in, but I am sure that once she decided that this was their life course the college administration didn't have a chance. Grandpa earned a Ph.D. in Education; Grandma typed his dissertation by hand (I can just picture her typing furiously away, and making whatever changes in it that she saw fit to make!). Grandma also entered college and graduated with an M.A. in English literature.

In 1954 Grandpa was hired by the U.S. Department of State to set up schools throughout the Middle East for the purpose of educating the rural populace, and off they flew. They were first posted to Lebanon, at that time known as the Paris of the Middle East. Later they were posted to Turkey, and then to Iran to do the same job. Grandma taught in the schools that Grandpa set up for the women, teaching English and westernized childrearing and housewifery practices.

Grandma loved it! During their time off they traveled extensively in Europe, Africa, and particularly the Middle East. When my grandparents did infrequently return to the U.S. they would show us slides of their trips; short stout Grandma staring haughtily down from the back of a camel in front of a pyramid (how in the world did they hoist her up there?), Grandpa grinning and shaking hands with the Shah of Iran.

Grandma treasured their life abroad and cherished the people that she met there. She made lifelong friends in every country she visited, and after her years overseas she entertained at home in a very cosmopolitan way. Because of her attitude the rest of our family all learned to not only accept "foreigners", but to value and enjoy diverse company. Grandma and Grandpa's home was a museum of lovely pieces from everywhere; real Persian carpets, fascinating African fossils, intricate silver Moroccan trays, fragile ancient vases carefully hand-carried back to America from the remote and dusty hills of Afghanistan, and vibrant, dazzling jewels (Grandma had a weakness for jewelry and her plump hands were always adorned with colorful sparkling rings).

I wasn't overly fond of Grandma when I was growing up; I was terrified of her for the most part. She never baked cookies for me, or played games with me, or did any of the things that my friends' grandparents did. Mostly she was just not around.

When Grandma was here in the flesh, she would eye me critically, demand that I speak up, and sharply query me about school and why I wasn't the best in my class. She would cast a censorious eye on whatever childish thing I was doing (and I seemed to always be doing something awkward and childish in front of her) and then she would sniff and inform me disapprovingly "You are a Kerwin; you can do better." Yikes! Even as a competent and successful adult I was always ever so slightly intimidated by her.

But when Grandma wasn't here, she ignited my imagination. I eagerly checked my mailbox to find her exciting postcards with the unfamiliar and romantic foreign stamps, and I marveled at the odd little toys that accompanied them, pouring through our back issues of National Geographic to try to visualize where they had come from. The mysteriousness and glamour of these items would send my thoughts soaring around the world, and I would play with the gifts that she sent me, daydreaming about all the alien and thrilling places that Grandma was visiting.

As I matured, I realized how astonishing Grandma's life really was. Born and raised in a time and place where women were expected to be content to stay home and knit (and Grandma actually did become an expert knitter after she retired), she instead roamed the world open to adventure, and she helped to change the course of world history.

Grandma didn't stop there! Among her many other accomplishments, she also published a children's book, earned awards for recording textbooks for the blind, painstakingly labeled her large and exquisite collection of Middle Eastern antiques, and loaned them out to local museums.

I grew to love and appreciate her, and as an adult became so proud of what she had achieved. I will never be as adventurous as she was, but in whatever I do I can feel Grandma looking disdainfully over my shoulder, sniffing critically, and telling me, "You can do better than that!" And I know that I can do it better, and I try again, harder.

Mary
By R.C. Van Horn

She never stopped being beautiful. Even after her hands started to shake, her lips, her legs, her whole being moving to a song we couldn't hear. Everything changed, really, as she stayed beautiful. Her hair slipped from black to peppered to white. Her smell, like the inside of a chest left in the attic, lingered years after she was gone. Her cheeks were soft, you could tell without touching, and flushed at the slightest thought. Her fingers were nimble, pianist's hands. And her eyes shifted between blue and gray, as she looked at you and stroked your face.

"We're alive," her touch seemed to say. "Isn't it strange?"

She wasn't supposed to have lived, my grandmother. Her heart was weak, leaving her with a lifetime of asthma attacks and trips to the hospital. But that was like her, too, defying expectations. On the one hand she was a breakable poet from Iowa: thin, reserved, melancholic. On the other hand she was a warrior wordsmith from the Midwest, pounding away at the typewriter and chaining herself to trees. She played Bach sonatas as if they were going to escape. She taught an 80-year-old man to read using the Bible, fulfilling his life-long dream while decrying the system that left him illiterate. She didn't take up much room, that Mary, but you could always tell where she had been. Watch out for the poets, she seemed to say, no matter how many dinners went uncooked for the sake of a stanza. Because that was the other thing about Mary: all her life she wanted the impossible.

She never stopped loving her husband, even after they divorced, even after he died. She never stopped wishing for her children to be happy, even after separations and alcoholism and poverty. She never stopped fighting for an end to war, even after Germany and Vietnam and Bosnia and Iraq. She lived inside her yearning like others live inside a cave, quiet and dry but ultimately unsatisfying. She needed the sun. She needed rain. Other people's worship could do little to placate the part of her still pounding away at the piano keys. What comfort she found was in her belief that humanity would fold into its capacity for love. And in the end, in those final moments when her body ceded to that which had been calling it all along, she lay surrounded by her children. And she said to them, "God is love, God is love." And her words filled the room.

Grandma's Promise Box
By Theresa Elders

Grandma frowned when she spied me on her porch, overstuffed pillowcase in hand. It was the summer of 1948 and I'd taken two buses and a streetcar from southwest Los Angeles, to her place near Sunset and Alvarado. That's a long journey for a girl of eleven, so I'd expected a hug and a grin, not a grimace.

"What's the matter, Grandma? You knew I was coming."

"Oh, child, I wish you weren't hauling your stuff around in that old sack."

I'd cut slits in the edges of the pillowcase, and fashioned a handle from purple yarn to tie the sides together. I'd brought underwear, a dress for Sunday at the Angelus Temple, and a library book, Noel Streatfield's *Ballet Shoes*, plus my flannel nightgown and slippers. I thought I'd done a good job.

"Didn't you ask for an overnight case for your birthday?" Grandma asked, leading me inside.

"Oh, I got a pair of roller skates. Mama worries about me taking the bus. Maybe she thinks I'm too young for a suitcase. Anyway, I love my skates. I can skate backwards now. I might ask again at Christmas."

My parents disliked what they called Grandma's cramped and musty apartment. I'd overheard Mama asking Daddy if it were safe for me to walk around downtown Los Angeles on those weekends I went to his mother's. They claimed the Westlake neighborhood was rundown, shabby, but I believed Grandma lived at the corner of Happiness and Bliss. At least monthly I'd spend the weekend.

Grandma put her kettle on to boil and sighed. She always welcomed me with a cup of tea, winter or summer. I'd feel very grownup as we nibbled toast with marmalade and sipped sugared tea, garnished with slices from lemons that grew in her backyard.

When the kettle whistled, Grandma poured boiling water into her delicate bone china teapot, gold-rimmed, and splashed with hand-painted burgundy roses. Then she handed me a little Scripture card holder, shaped like a loaf of bread, with "Bread of Life" written across the side.

"While I toast the bread, rummage through the Promise Box and see if you can find a verse you'd like to say for our grace."

The first one I pulled out seemed fitting.

"Listen, Grandma. This Scripture is about me traveling to see you. It's from Psalms. 'The Lord will keep you from all harm—he will watch over your life. The Lord will watch over your coming and going both now and forevermore.' "

Grandma smiled. "Well, the Lord will watch over you. And your Grandma will, too. Just wait and you'll see." She handed me a slice of buttered toast.

We sat companionably, planning the next day's excursions. Sundays we'd always take a short walk to the bus stop to catch a ride to the Angelus Temple. In the afternoon we'd feed swans in Echo Park, or ride the paddle boats at MacArthur Park. Sometimes we'd watch a matinee at the corner movie theater or soak in the salt water at Bimini Baths. Some sultry summer afternoons we'd simply loll around in the garden behind her old Victorian apartment building, picking lemons to slice for our tea and sampling Concord grapes from an overgrown vine.

"Child, why don't you wash up? I'm going downstairs to the storage unit for something. You can pick a fresh dish towel."

I delighted in sorting through the embroidered towels in her kitchen drawer. This time I found one with a cow jumping over the moon and used it to pat dry the delicate teapot. Just as I finished hanging our cups on the hooks under her dish cabinet, I heard Grandma trudging back up the stairs behind me.

It must have been a miracle. When I turned around, I
spied a mahogany brown overnight case, with a leather
handle and gold hardware, sitting on the kitchen table.

"Your cousin Patricia left this here a while back. She
called it her train case. I don't think she needs it anymore."

Grandma lifted the lid to reveal an embedded mirror,
and stretch straps on the fawn lining, which I guessed could
hold perfume or shampoo bottles and brushes.

"It will do just as well for buses and streetcars as it
would for a train."

"Oh, Grandma," I cried. "It's perfect."

"I keep my promises," Grandma said. "I promised
you'd always have the Lord and me looking out for you."

Glowing with gratitude, I transferred the contents of my
old pillowcase into my adorable new piece of genuine
leatherette luggage. That night, after reading another chapter
of *Ballet Shoes,* I thanked Grandma in my bedtime prayers for
both Patricia's train case, and for assuring me that the Lord
always would watch over me.

I carried that case around for years. Much later, long
after Grandma died, I used it to store mementoes of my
childhood and adolescence: autograph books, majorette
award ribbons, menus and corsages from teenage dates and
dances. And even the little Bread of Life Promise Box
Grandma gave me for my wedding.

Then one desolate day in my late twenties, my son ran
into the apartment where we lived, yelling that the garages
were on fire. When we'd moved from a larger place, we'd
stored a lot of items in that garage. That fire destroyed our
dining room table, a Singer sewing machine, several boxes of
books... and my overnight case.

I grieved the case the most.

Now, a widowed grandmother myself, I'm alone in the
country with my dogs and cats. My own grandchildren live far
away, so can't hop on a bus or streetcar to visit me. I suppose
there's no need for a Bread of Life box, so a child could
search for an appropriate blessing.

But still, out of curiosity I Googled "promise box" and found one that's up for auction on eBay. It looks just like the one Grandma gave me half a century ago.

I bid on it. I can always use a blessing… and the box will remind me that Grandma and the Lord keep their promises.

Grandma Martha
By Suzan L. Wiener

In the Spring of 1956, mom and I took the train when I was a young girl of ten, and visited Grandma Martha every Saturday, rain or shine. We lived in the Bronx at the time, and the ride was an hour long. I used to get quite fidgety sitting in my seat, trying not to stare at all the other passengers.

Grandma Martha was beautiful but even I could see she was quite weak. She had cataracts, and I remember how she would always sit with tea bags on her eyes to sooth the pain. She took the tea bags off to see her "Susie" as she called me. Grandma Martha wore her gray hair in a bun, and she was a bit overweight. Mom told me Grandma Martha was somber with her, but was always jolly to me, and the way she paid attention to me was a godsend, since I was mostly ignored by others

She would say, "Oh, pretty girl, Susie," and give me a big hug. She made me feel special. I enjoyed her company and looked forward to the chocolate bar she gave me. Grandma Martha never forgot that. We had the love of chocolate in common.

Unfortunately, the flu she had gotten the week before had knocked her for a loop. The doctor told Mom that her immune system wasn't good and she would need to rest. We were all worried about her, and hoped for the best since Grandma Martha was about to turn 80 years-old.

Saturday was Grandma's birthday. We were thinking of having a birthday party for her, with all the relatives, but knew that would be too much excitement for her, so mom baked her a delicious chocolate cake with white icing.

At the last minute, I changed my mind. I asked if I could go to the roller rink with my friends instead of Grandma's party. Mom agreed and drove me there. She said she would explain it to Grandma, but I still felt guilty anyway. I had a fairly nice time with my friends, but I missed Grandma a lot. After a short while, I decided to go home. When I got home, Grandma was waiting for me outside.

"What are you doing here?" I asked happily and quite surprised. She seldom left her apartment because she had so much trouble walking. It was cold, but Grandma didn't mind. Her smile was so bright. I had never seen her so happy. The walk didn't make her tired or achy either. Reaching our house, I asked if she was going to stay for dinner.

"I can't sweetheart," she replied. "I have to go, but know I love you." She took out a chocolate bar from her pocket and gave it to me.

"I'm sorry I wasn't with you for your birthday," I said, hugging her.

Grandma Martha looked warmly at me, then waved goodbye. "No problem at all, my pretty girl, Susie." I loved when she said that to me. I watched her walk away until I couldn't see her anymore.

When I went inside, my mother was in tears and when I asked what was wrong, she told me Grandma had passed away. I was stunned and started crying.

"But, Mom, I was just with her. She walked me home just a little while ago. She even gave me this chocolate bar," I said, showing her.

"It's okay, honey, Mom replied, "I know Grandma meant a lot to you.

My mother didn't believe I had really seen Grandma but it didn't matter. Grandma and I knew the truth. She had come to say goodbye, and to let me know that she wasn't angry with me.

In November of 1973, when I married my husband Howard, I would often tell him how Grandma Martha came to me that day. He knew I wasn't crazy. He could see by my hurt and tears I was telling the truth. He listened intently, holding my hand to show how much he cared. He would always say he could see how much my Grandmother Martha meant to me. I love you, Grandma Martha. Thank you for loving me.

Loose Seams
By Gabriella Brand

I am sitting on two Manhattan telephone books so I can reach the table. My grandmother's eggplant is on a large porcelain platter. It is 1953. I watch as the dark purple pile makes its way around the room. The dish is being passed from grandfather to father, from uncle to aunt, from aunt to cousin. It is one of my grandmother's specialties.

I feel certain I will gag.

"Can I be excused?" I ask.

No one hears me. An uncle is holding forth about the New York Yankees, what Mickey Mantle did at the bottom of the ninth. My grandmother is rushing back and forth from the dining room to the kitchen like a human shuttle, in and out, weaving dinner, bringing forth more and more food. My father is telling a joke about Carnegie Hall. One of the aunts is raising her wine glass and laughing a little too loud.

"Excuse me," I try again, banging my polished Mary Janes against the rung of the chair.

The eggplant is coming closer. I try to get my mother's attention. Surely Mother will plead in my favor. Surely she will explain to her fierce mother-in-law, once again, that it's not easy having a finicky eater for a daughter.

But Mother has her head down. She is on the other side of the huge mahogany table with the lace tablecloth.

On the wall behind her is a framed painting of a long-haired man with his chest cut open like a window. The man has piercing eyes. He is exposing his heart. The heart itself is oversized. It is purplish and looks rather squishy. A cousin once told me that it was the Sacred Heart of Jesus. My parents don't go to church. There are no such paintings in our house. But I am not in my house. It's Sunday afternoon. We are visiting Grandma.

I try to get Father's attention. He's telling another version of his story about Carnegie Hall.

I look at that squishy heart and I look once again at the squishy eggplant. They are almost the same color. The room suddenly feels very hot. I fall head first onto the table, barely missing the little glass cruets of vinegar and oil and the plate of antipasto. Later, while I am recovering on the sofa in the living room with a little tartan-covered icepack on my head, Cousin Ponette will tiptoe in to report after dinner, Grandfather gave all the grandchildren crisp new two-dollar bills.

"You didn't get one. Because you messed up the table."

"I couldn't help it," I say.

I try to look sad and remorseful. But secretly I am delighted that I missed dinner. Once again.

It wasn't just eggplant, of course. Everything about my grandmother felt strange to me, the very fiber of her being— her beliefs, her talents, her tastes.

There's an old black and white home movie of me as a toddler. Grandma is determined to plant a kiss on my cheek. I shudder and pull away. She tries again. My lower lip trembles. My father, holding the camera, must have urged my older brother to come into the shot. My brother kisses me and I make no protest. Grandma tries again. My face contorts into disgust. The camera—no sound in those days—silently records my scream. Somewhere from the depths of Proustian memory, as I re-watch the old movie, I recall a nauseating odor of Chiclets gum mixed with Arpège perfume. It was my grandmother's signature smell.

As I grew up, the gap between us grew even wider. There were so many differences, a sense of style, for one thing. Grandma had magic fingers. She could take a piece of silk and turn it into a shawl, a scarf, a blouse or a caftan. Trained as a dressmaker, she could spot the small flaw in a man's suit, the loose seam in a woman's skirt.

I felt examined.

Whether I was wearing my prettiest party dress or a brand-new pair of Bermuda shorts, nothing ever met Grandma's standards.

"You shouldn't wear yellow," she said to me once. "It makes your skin look like the yolk of an egg."

When my breasts began to develop, I dreaded her scrutiny.

"You don't have enough bosom to wear an empire waist," she stated, disapprovingly. "It's a nice style for say, your cousin Ponette."

Once my grandmother lifted up the hem of one of my skirts, right there at the Oyster Bar in Grand Central Station, in full view of the waiters.

"Ugh," she said. "They skimped on the lining. No wonder it doesn't hang right. A lining gives the garment shape."

I protested. I thought the skirt looked just fine. But Grandma carried on.

"You can't see it. So you think it's not important. But, trust me, everything needs a lining."

The biggest difference between my grandmother and me was that she was all hands, and I was all head. At least back then.

Once, on a long car trip, she tried to teach me to knit. She, Mother, and I were ensconced in the wide back seat.

"Zip, zip, zip, "she said. "Cast on. Like this."

Each morning she'd open her knitting bag and hand me the uneven rows I had done the day before. But I could never remember which gaping hole the needle went through. She'd have to show me all over again.

Once she was making homemade ravioli. Not with a machine, but by manipulating a little cutting tool equipped with a zigzagged edge.

"Here. Sit. Learn to do this," she ordered.

Obediently. I hoisted myself on a kitchen stool. Had Grandma forgotten that I couldn't cut a straight line? That I had no sense of proportion? I watched cousin Ponette turn out one perfect little pocket after another. My grandmother took one look at my lopsided ravioli and immediately tried to scoop out the filling like a dental hygienist scraping plaque. Her face was stern. She released me from further duty. I was relieved and happy. For the remainder of the visit, I could now retreat to a quiet corner with a book.

Books, in fact, became the biggest barrier between us. I had been an early, hungry reader. More than once I tried to sneak books onto my lap at mealtimes. But it became clear that Grandma disapproved, somehow, of anything even remotely literary.

"You think story books tell you about life?" she said to me one day. "Well, life is what you live. Not what you read."

I didn't know how to answer her. I was sixteen. I was reading Emile Zola. Theodore Dreiser. Realism, wasn't it? I tried to defend myself, but my parents winked at me and I knew enough to stop.

Years later, I caught wind of a family secret. Grandmother couldn't read. People intimated that her immigrant parents in the late 1800s had kept her hidden under the sewing machine when the New York City truant office came around. It was said she had never attended school. This didn't prevent her from successfully working as a couturiere, negotiating in various languages, and even running her own business. Perhaps she hired others to do the reading and writing.

Today, long after my grandmother's death, I marvel at that tiny dynamo with so many skills, enormous energy and a sharp tongue. I wish I had learned things from her. How to fold a napkin so it looks like a bird. How to pull off wearing a flower in my hair. How to show grit in the face of challenge.

I'm a grandmother myself now. I realize that affinities between grandparents and grandchildren are mysterious and fragile things. No one knows what smells and fears and words might divide us or bond us forever. No one knows what we each need from the other. No one knows what we each can give.

I have no doubt that Grandma and I needed something from each other. Something that neither one of us could provide nor receive. Whatever it was, it was something important. Something like the lining of a dress. Something you couldn't see.

Granny Takes the Burnt Toast
By Stephanie Rose

My granny has always been the human embodiment of "grandma takes the burnt toast." She is the most selfless person I have ever known and I always aspire to be more like her in nature. She always puts other people first, whether they be family, friend or stranger.

When I was little, she often took care of me when I was sick, bringing me care packages of Lucozade, lemonade and rich tea biscuits (for some reason, these were my cravings during illness). She would sit with me for hours without complaint, and give me things to keep me occupied and take my mind off my misery, even if it was something as simple as having me unwind the wool as she knitted beside me.

All throughout my life, anything of my granny's that I admired, she gave up for me. I have so many of her rings, and other assorted jewelry, including an antique ring that is beautifully engraved and has five rubies in a beautiful setting. I never take it off.

Perfume, wool dresses, CDs and CD players, old music sheets, you name it; she has parted with it all.

When we ask why she so readily gives up her possessions for us, she simply replies, "They're just things to me. I'd quite happily watch someone else enjoy them."

Recently, I happened to comment on the lovely color of the scarf she was wearing as she left our house, and straight away, she whipped it from her neck and handed it to me.

"Here. Take it," she insisted, then joked, "Look at me. Giving you the clothes off my back!"

She is a self-proclaimed witch with her "evil eye" and "ugly thumb." Her so-called evil eye could see all and she would often predict events with a shout of, "See! I told you! I'm a witch!" whenever any of her "premonitions" came true.

As for her thumb, she got it caught in a mangle as a child, leaving it permanently deformed, and thus, she had always dubbed it her "ugly thumb." Somehow, I could never be repulsed by it, because it was attached to my wonderful granny.

She even used her witches' powers to help me stand up to bullies when I was growing up (her heart was in the right place).

At the very mention of me being picked on, she would say, "Well, you know what to do. Tell them I'm a witch," or, "Tell them I'll come and put the evil eye on them," or, more embarrassingly, "Tell them your big, fat granny will come and squash them!"

I say it was embarrassing for the simple fact that I took her advice. How was I to know the bullies would only laugh harder? I laugh too in hindsight.

My little cousin and I have always been particularly close to Granny, as she often babysat us together, and she and my granda (grandfather) were always taking us on beach holidays in their caravan or on day trips to the zoo and other such places. Somehow, she never once, in all our years, lost her temper with us, no matter how annoying we were. Messing her hair, pinging her stockings, giving her lip and just generally being the "cheeky, wee monkeys" that we were.

She had endless patience for us and she provided countless activities to keep us entertained—baking, making pom-poms, picnics on the stairs and, our personal favorite, cooking sausages on the beach. Even on day-outings, she would produce snacks, notebooks and puzzles from her "magic bag." Those years spent with them were some of the best of my life.

One memory of my granny stands out in particular. I was very young and my mum and I were visiting my granny just after Valentine's Day. It was a visit like any other but just before we were leaving, my granny stopped us with a "Hold on. I've got something for you."

She went through to the kitchen and came back with a beautiful handcrafted, hand-painted box filled with Valentine's candies, apparently from my "secret admirer."

"It came through the door for you," she told me. "They must have known that I was your granny and that you'd be coming here."

I loved it. It made me feel so special, and for a long time I would remember it and find myself wondering who this mysterious suitor was.

It didn't occur to me until years later that my granny was my secret admirer. Even once that I realized it was her, it didn't bother me because to be honest, I'm her secret admirer too.

Life in Full Circle
By Jamie Grabert

We refer to my grandmother as "The Rock." She didn't earn this title until my grandfather was in the midst of being consumed by Alzheimer's. To some she seems ordinary, but to the community who knows her, she's extraordinary.

We've always had a special bond. I'm the first granddaughter, and therefore, the guinea pig. I'm also twenty-five percent my mother, and seventy-five percent her mother, which makes our story great. My father's mother calls me "Little Opal," a statement I take to heart as a compliment.

As a small child growing up in rural Southern Indiana, there was no place I would have rather been than on my grandparents' farm. That is home. Gram Opal made it that way, not just for her children and grandchildren, but also for friends, family, and neighbors of all shapes and sizes. She had a knack for taking care of people, always acting the role of the gracious host, even when she would have rather been relaxing on her front porch swing admiring the jungle that we planted with her every Mother's Day.

When she was a young adult, just before marrying my grandfather, she served as a nanny, to a young family with a boy with disabilities. As her parents and my grandfather's parents began to age and need help caring for themselves, my grandmother always stepped in to care for them. My mom and I would help out too. When I broke bones, had reconstructive knee surgeries, a broken heart or even a sore throat, Gram stood back, waiting for mom to let her take over.

At home she backed whatever my Grandfather said, except when it came to me. I was, and still am, the exception to every rule. She privately and unassumingly voiced her practical wisdom, until he heard the message. But no one knew or at least acknowledged her quiet determination.

Their relationship went on like that for years, until the Long Good-Bye began. Her leadership began to take on a new role. Her dominance in the family began to come to light. Slowly at first, and then more quickly, she became the leader in the family, but she still managed to maintain her servant heart. She didn't weep. She didn't get upset. She didn't feel sorry for herself or allow my grandfather to feel sorry for himself.

At seventy-seven years of age, she took on the care of my grandfather, who became more and more child-like. Gone were the days of running to the mall on a whim with her sister-in-law, his sister (who had developed Alzheimer's). Gone were the days of taking trips with their friends and teaching Sunday school classes, which he had done for decades. Gone was the life she knew. She stopped caring for herself and focused solely on him.

Washing his clothes, changing him often, trying to wrestle him for a shower, watching him take all of his meds (he liked to hide them in the furniture and would often offer them to visitors with a grin), making him eat as close to balanced meals as she could when all he wanted to eat was sweets, were just a few of her daily tasks. Yet, somehow, she still cared for the rest of us. Rarely did she miss a birthday or anniversary. The cards would still show up in the mail, perhaps a day early or late, but she always remembered. Flowers and donations were sent for funerals. If she heard about a sick friend or loved one, she would call them regularly to see how they were doing. She took over paying the bills, gathering the information for taxes, organizing meds, scheduling doctor appointments, and on and on.

I spent one day a week caring for him, so she could have some time to feel normal again. At first, she would go freely to run errands, but as his condition worsened, she would not leave his side. When I arrived, I would ask how things have been and what I was in for that day.

She would smile, and say, "Your grandpa's in there somewhere. I saw a glimpse of him. That was all I needed.

We can't give up. We can't cry. He's still here, and that's what's important."

I saw the way the disease took its toll on her, mentally and physically. She went from being an active senior citizen to taking long naps. She would tell me how she was just getting a few hours here and there because he had become something of an escape artist, and she was afraid he would take off in the middle of the night. One time she told me he tried to go home with another lady at the grocery. Grandpa didn't stay home much longer after that. It was getting harder and harder to care for him. Inside she knew it was coming, but she didn't have the heart to put him in a nursing home.

On one of my visits, I noticed Gram was quieter than normal. Her pep talk was very brief. She just wanted to sit in the living room with him and watch television. She was content, so he was content. I decided to help by cleaning. My concern grew. When she didn't come in the kitchen and talk to me, I knew something was wrong. This went on for a few days. She went to the doctor, and it was discovered that she'd had a mini-stroke.

It was time for Grandpa to go to the nursing home. The hardships of taking care of him at home had become too much for her. Her children fought over it, mostly from the guilt they had of not being there, or feeling helpless for their parents and perhaps acknowledging for the first time that Superman and Wonder Woman had chinks in their armor.

Gram never faltered. She continued to lead the family through this tough time. It was in this time that we discovered she had been the rock that held the family together. Our strength came from seeing how she continuously faced adversity and never stopped pushing forward. She didn't cry. She made us laugh. She told us stories about how my grandpa had swept her off her feet and stole her from another man. She reminded us of happy times with him and told us to remember him the way he was.

I took Gram to visit grandpa on their anniversary, which also happened to be Mother's Day. It would also end up being their last anniversary, as he passed on a few months later. While we were there, for the first time in years, he called her by her middle name, which he often did as a term of endearment. Just before we left, she kissed him on the forehead, and told him she loved him.

He responded, "Lena, I always did like you."

He held her shaking hand in his, and told her he loved her. We drove home quietly, and she softly wept.

In hospice, she made sure the family was there twenty-four hours a day. She brought us together. She would argue every night that she should stay. But we would find the courage to make her go. For eight days, she sat by his side. She would tell him who was there for a visit. She patted his arm. She held his hand. When his breathing began to slow late on his last afternoon, I stood by her side, holding her up with my aunt and uncle on the other side of the bed. He looked right at her, unable to speak, but trying.

She looked at him and said, "I always did like you, too."

That was all he needed to hear.

When my grandpa died, she was the gracious hostess at the viewing and when people brought food to the farm to offer their condolences. She offered them her seat. She would comfort them. She graciously thanked those who came. She seemed to never get tired.

For the last three years, she remained on the farm. She kept up with her flowers and pets, with the help of my uncle, and hung out on her porch, a post-grandpa gift that came as the result of him burning the garage down around her car. I still helped one day a week for a while, but soon became busy with my work. I learned a number of new things about her in that time. She was smarter than she let anyone see. She was highly aware of current events and was politically-minded, something we never knew.

Gradually, Gram became ill. She stopped caring for herself almost completely. She felt as if she was a burden, so she didn't tell anyone how bad she had been feeling. My mom and aunt called and asked me to check on her. I did. But she didn't want me to come for a visit, so I knew something was wrong. I had taken a mental inventory of what I noticed and called her doctor, who sent us to the emergency room.

She spent the next three weeks in the hospital. We discovered how serious her condition had become. She now had non-alcohol-induced cirrhosis of the liver and was in all-out kidney failure. We were told a number of times she may go at any time. They told us that it was a matter of what would give out first—her body or her will.

They didn't know Gram. She will not "go gently into that good night." It was in her struggle to bounce back we saw who she really is. Her quick wit and love still filled the room. Today, she goes to dialysis three days a week and attends group physical therapy sessions five days a week at her assisted living facility. She goes to Bingo, and mercilessly strives to win, although she says she's just doing it for fun. Everyone loves her, probably because she loves them.

In a recent trip to the doctor, Gram told me she didn't remember much about her time in the hospital. She asked a few questions, and I answered. She told me she felt like a bad mother because she put us through all of that. Again, she put us before herself.

I responded with something she taught us all, "Gram, that doesn't make you a bad mother. You made us come together. We are staying closer and working together to take care of you. You battled back in spite of what the doctors told us. You taught us about miracles and fighting back. You're a great mother and grandmother. Don't ever feel bad about that."

She thanked me for caring for her. I explained that I was merely following her example. She asked me if I remembered that Disney movie with the lions. I nodded. She responded, "Well, this is the circle of life. You take care of others like you have been cared for yourself. Do it in love, not obligation, and you will be blessed."

Lighting Up With Alice
By Kristina Jensen

"Hi," I said without looking up. I was kneeling on the floor in my room doing cartoon sketches with a blue ballpoint pen. I was wearing the brand new Muppet T-shirt that my aunt had given me for my eighth birthday and my new red shorts. I knew Alice had come in because everything went kind of cold for a second, as if a fridge door had been opened in my room.

"Hello," Alice said as she peered over my shoulder. I knew again, without looking, that Alice was wearing that same old-fashioned black dress, high collared with lace at the cuffs and little lace up boots that went half way up her calves.

"What is that?" she asked, "that thing you have in your hand?"

"It's called a ball point pen," I said, holding it up so Alice could see it.

"How do you fill it up?"

"What? Fill it up?"

"How does the ink get into it?"

"It's inside it already, when Mum buys it. When it runs out you get a new one. You want to have a go?"

"Yes, I would please."

I made room on the floor and got out a clean sheet of paper for Alice. Alice sat down, arranging her skirts so they were out of the way. She took the pen gingerly, holding it between finger and thumb as if it might bite and made a long straight line on the paper with the pen.

"That's enough," she said frowning and handing the pen back. "I don't want to run it out."

"Oh no, silly, it won't run out for ages. Go on. Draw something else," I said. "Look, I've got another one. I'll draw too."

We carried on in silence for a few minutes. I continued filling up my page with funny eye and nose combinations.

"What are you drawing, Alice?" I asked. I couldn't see what she was doing because her neat blond ringlets were hanging down like a curtain over her hand as she drew. Alice had dark blue ribbons in her hair today. It was always so tidy, so perfect. I self-consciously ran my fingers through my own pageboy bird's nest.

"Oh, it's nothing really. It's not very good. I like those funny people you're drawing though. They look like insects." Alice sat up straight and revealed a very life-like blue pen sketch of a bunch of violets surrounded by a nest of leaves.

"Wow! That is awesome. I didn't know you could draw like that."

"Well," Alice said, "I love violets. They are my favorite flower and Mother encourages us to do nature studies. She says it gives one an appreciation of beauty." Alice always spoke like that. It reminded me of the accents of English kids in the Disney Sunday movies on TV.

"Me too," I said. Thinking about violets always reminded me of my Gar, my very much adored, tiny white-haired grandmother who had passed away last year just before I turned seven. In her garden, their tiny purple faces had peeped out from under every camellia bush. Mum had transplanted a patch of those same violets to our garden and I was allowed to pick them whenever I liked.

"Hey, you want to play that game with the lights again, like we did last time?" I asked Alice.

"In the wardrobe?" Alice looked at me with a little sideways grin on her face. Alice didn't smile much but she looked very pretty when she did. She had a little dimple that only showed when she smiled.

I wondered if I could ever be pretty like Alice. Dad said I was pretty dirty when I had asked him if he thought I was pretty. At the time, I had dirt on my knees and face from playing down in the drain so this was true, but Dad had laughed as he had said it, so I think he was only joking. My brother had of course chipped in and said that I was pretty ugly but I didn't care really what he said.

It might be nice to get dressed up like Alice, I thought, though I didn't know if I'd want to have to lace up those boots. What if I wanted to take them off and run in the grass? It would be dark before I'd even get one off.

I rummaged around in the wardrobe, making a space in the toy debris. Big Teddy lay sprawled out with a hole in his tummy, stuffing oozing out: the result of a doctor game that my brother and I had played last week. Various body parts of other toys lay in confused heaps in the corners, tossed together with my clothes and shoes. We squeezed in, Alice's skirts rustling as she sat down. I pulled the door shut with the special piece of string attached to the handle and Alice made the lights.

First she made the little globes, each one about the size of a marble. They hung on the bottoms of Mum's old dancing skirts and on Dad's jackets that he said were from when he was 'young and foolish'.

"Cool," I breathed, "can you make those ones in your hair like last time?"

Alice smiled again in the dark and I saw her teeth glow in the light from the balls. Slowly, like glowworms lighting up, little fairy lights began to sparkle in Alice's hair.

"Me too, please?" I whispered.

Alice's hair was on fire with the tiny specks of silver light. I wanted them in my hair too. Maybe they would make me pretty like Alice.

Alice raised her hand until her palm was directly above my head. Little light dots started falling out of her palm onto my head, and I covered my eyes with my hands and gasped.

"It's all right, they don't hurt, remember?" Alice giggled. I opened my eyes and Alice flicked her fingers and all the lights leapt up off our heads and began to flutter around like bright little bugs.

"Look," Alice said and she opened her mouth and stuck out the little pink tip of her tongue. A speck of light landed on it and made a tiny crackling sound.

"You try it," she said. I caught one straight away on my tongue and jumped when a miniscule burst of smoke puffed up right in front of my eyes. It was like a flea-sized firecracker. It tickled and I laughed, which set Alice off too. She put her hand over her mouth but it was too late. We got the giggles and couldn't stop.

Suddenly, I felt a vibration under my bottom. Footsteps were coming down the hall. I grabbed Alice's arm, the stiff fabric of her dress felt cool and papery under my fingers.

"Rachel? Where are you? Who are you talking to?"

It was Mum.

"Rachel? Have you got your torch on in the wardrobe again?"

I stopped breathing and put a finger to my lips. Alice nodded, her face serious now. She tugged my hand towards hers so that our palms were almost touching. As Mum tugged the door open, she put our hands together and the lights went out.

"Ah, there you are," Mum said. "I could hear you laughing. Sounded like you were sharing a great old joke with someone."

I let out my breath and took a big sniff in and that's when I smelt the smell. It came from Alice.

Mum started moving around the room picking up some of my clothes off the floor and folding them. "Thought I'd better check that Andrea hadn't turned up here again without telling her mother where she was. And what were you doing with your torch on in there? I've told you before not to waste the batteries."

"Yes Mum," I said.

I looked at Alice. Alice looked back, her eyes wide.

"Now, exactly what are you up to?" said Mum, turning around, hands on her hips with a frown on her face.

"I was just talking to Alice, Mum." I looked up into my mother's face.

"Oh yes, Alice, well that's nice dear. Now come on, get your farm clothes on. Dad's waiting with the tractor. We're going up into the paddock by the old house to see if we can find any mushrooms for dinner while he shifts the bulls. Bring your jumper, okay, it might get chilly."

And Mum walked out.

I crawled out of the wardrobe to the pile of old farm clothes on the floor near my bed. I spoke with my jersey stuck half way over my head, "Hey Alice, why don't you come back when I've finished getting the mushrooms. We can do some more… "

But when my head popped through the too-tight hole, I saw that Alice had gone.

"… drawing."

That strange smell was gone too.

I got my old trousers on, found my gumboots in the pile on the back step, and raced out to the tractor.

"Mum? Have we still got the old dress up box?" I asked as I scrambled up to sit on the tire guard next to Dad.

"Yes," yelled Mum over the noise of the tractor, "it's up in the hall cupboard."

"That's probably where those rats have been nesting," said Dad, winking at me.

"Why?" asked Mum, "you haven't played with those things for a couple of years now."

"Is there any stuff that used to belong to Gar in there?" I asked, hanging on tight as we bumped across the cattle stop.

"I think it's all Alice's stuff plus a couple of my old dresses," said Mum, leaning across behind Dad so she didn't have to shout. "Why do you want to get it down?"

"What?" I said, staring at my mother.

What did she say? Alice's stuff?

"Who's Alice, Mum?"

"Alice was my mother's name, your Gar, remember?" Mum replied, eyes forward on the track looking out for the ruts that could tumble us off.

My heart skipped a beat, then doubled up on itself and jumped up into my mouth. Alice. My Gar. My grandmother.

My thoughts felt as though they were bouncing inside my head as Dad wove the tractor along the track. That morning, I had been reminded of Gar when Alice drew the violets and I had noticed that her clothes smelled. It had been such a familiar scent that a pain in my heart went straight to the place where Gar lived. I had virtually stayed with her every weekend until I was six so that Mum could have some time out. Gar would arrive after school each Friday and pick me up, and take me home again on Sunday afternoon. We would have tea parties with the faeries under the sprawling Japanese maple and I would sleep in the matching twin bed in Gar's room.

"I just want to look at them again," I said.

"Let's get them down when we get home, ay?" said Dad, "and you and Mum can get all dolled up and give me a fashion show. How about it, Mum? Think you can still squeeze into that little turquoise number?"

Mum gave Dad a playful punch in the arm and they both laughed.

"Can we, Mum?" I said, feeling that I simply had to push my nose into one of Gar's dresses just to make sure.

Soon we were up at the old house picking mushrooms but I couldn't concentrate and when it was time to go, I only had a few in the bottom of my bucket. I kept thinking about Alice and the smell and hoped Dad would hurry up so we could go home and get the box down.

Mum took her boots off, dumping the mushroom buckets down in the kitchen.

"Can we get it down now, Mum?" I asked, "the dress up box, remember?" I felt a sort of desperation inside. I wanted to find out if my hunch was right.

"After I get the dinner on, okay?" said Mum.

"Oh please, can you get it down now? Can I get it?" I pleaded, hopping from one foot to the other.

Mum took a deep breath. "No, I'll get it down. I don't want you climbing up there and breaking your neck. Get the little step ladder out of the laundry for me."

Finally the box sat on the floor in the middle of my room.

"Look out for those rats," Mum said, "I'm going to get dinner started."

I shut the door. I didn't even have to open the box to know that my little inkling was right.

Picking up the dress that lay crumpled on top, I buried my nose in it. Gar's smell oozed out from fabric patterned with tiny blue roses: Alice's smell.

Author's Note:

My grandmother died when I was nearly seven and I still recall the sad angry feelings that coursed through me when I came home from school and Mum told me that she had been to Gar's funeral that day.

No one seemed to understand how upset I was at not being able to see her while she was dying of pancreatic cancer or go to her funeral.

Not long after, I began to 'see' a little girl, usually in my room, dressed in a long sleeved dark colored dress with lace at the collar and lace up boots. She spoke to me and we played together, often interrupted by my mother who would come to see who it was I was talking to.

Years later, as my teenage me helped my mother put some old family pictures into frames, I was shocked to see a photo of my 'imaginary friend', as Mum used to call her. 'Who is that?' I asked and she replied, 'That's my mother, Alice, your Gar.'

Until that moment, I had not put my imaginary friend's name and my Gar's name together and I wondered maybe if she had come back to me to keep me company, knowing I would miss her terribly. She has appeared to me on two other occasions, both in churches at funerals, and her presence encouraged me to feel not sadness but a deep joy and a realization that we never really lose someone we love.

So this story is a mixture of fact and fiction but the lights were very, very real.

Decatur Girl
by Karen Warinsky

Talcum powder, chin whiskers, hatboxes, powdered donuts, bingo, cigarette cough, hugs and whispers. Those words do describe my Grandma Baker. Thinking more, I come up with dictionary, crossword puzzles, apron, rolled silk stockings, Cuban heels and costume jewelry.

I am one of her namesakes, and supposedly (according to my mother) her favorite grandchild. Even my cousin Steve agrees with that, and if I am her favorite, then Steve is second. She had 14 grandchildren from her two sons and three daughters, and paid close attention to them all. My brother and I really only saw her twice a year after we moved up north, but for the first five years of my life she was a weekly fixture, our closeness coming from that early time. She always had a book and a crossword going. She told of hiding under her bed with a book as a child while her Mama hollered, "Grace, come here and help your sisters!" Housework in that era was demanding; rugs to beat, vacuum cleaners to pump by hand, clothes to wash in a tub on the porch with a scrub board, and meal after meal to prepare.

Grace's mother would have been right to demand help from her girls. But my Grandma was never one to take a crazed pride in the cleanliness of her house, preferring to read, visit, or watch television to giving the floors a good waxing, unlike my Grandma Lockett who made everything crisp and spotless as if to make a point to the world. I have inherited a strange mix of these traits as I love to read and relax but can only do it once the place is organized and clean.

During the Great Depression when Grace had already read all the books in the tiny Roodhouse, Illinois library, and had no money or ability to go anywhere or do anything else, she would just sit and read the dictionary. My mother has vivid memories of coming home from school and seeing her lost in thought with the big dictionary in her lap. I remember snuggling next to her plump, flabby, cotton-clad form on my parent's cheap 1950s couch, as she read story after story to me. Books were her lifeline, and part of her legacy to me is her small, suede bound copy of The Rubaiyat, by Omar Khayyam, the copy given to her by her early love, a man named Charles Drake.

She loved to tease, and one favorite tale is of her walking in her stocking feet down the sidewalk one bright spring day, secretly following her oldest daughter Florence, then 16. With unkempt hair, a rough blanket thrown over her shoulders and no shoes, Grandma was quite a sight. Florence was on her way to meet a boy, and when she sensed something strange and turned around to see her mother looking like a beggar woman, she screamed and hurried off, leaving Grace laughing. Grace owned a dog for a while whose name was "Guess," and she enjoyed the perplexed looks on faces when innocent passersby asked the animal's name and were continually told to "Guess." (Boxer? Fido? Rex?) Grace became heavy in mid-life, and as an old woman when she lost the weight her body sagged.

I remember playing with the loose flesh of her under arms when she was old, patting them back and forth. She tolerated this and other indignities. Seemingly without ego she loved to make us laugh at her expense, clacking her false teeth, mugging and making goofy faces. She indulged our curiosity about the wide variety of moles on her back and torso that we would see when she changed her dress, or got ready for bed. Nothing was off limits. She was a hug machine and always ready to be sat upon, next to, have her hair brushed and to be loved.

Born in 1890 in Decatur, Illinois, Grace had three older brothers and was the middle of three sisters. Her early world was one of pretense and attempted outer elegance for girls and women, with fussy dresses and petticoats, hats and gloves that were required in public. Her girlhood journal is pasted full of magazine ads she cut out showing typical scenes of

attractive young men with their arms around small-waisted
girls with mounds of luscious hair piled atop their heads. The
pasted pictures show everything about the fashion of the day
that   a   young   girl   would   find   interesting.

High-minded, she copied with a fountain pen in a steady,
rounded hand, verses of poetry, a quote from a "Rev.
Beecher," presumably Henry Ward Beecher, the minister
brother of Harriet Beecher Stowe, several long "dates to
remember," and comments about friends. The Beecher
quote states: "Of all earthly music that which reaches farthest
into heaven is the beating of a loving heart." The notation is
"G.M.B.W., June 16, 1906," standing for Grace Margaret
Booth Williams. The name Booth was chosen by her mother
to honor the founders of the Salvation Army, William and
Catherine Booth.

Hers was a working class family. Her father John
Williams, a bugle boy in the Civil War, was a carpenter who
built his own home, and her mother, Mattie Lynn Williams,
was a tiny woman of Irish-English extraction whose family
came to Illinois from Virginia in a covered wagon, a small
library of books tucked in among the supplies. Mattie ran the
busy household firmly and with Christian values. By all
accounts they were mostly happy, entertaining themselves by
popping corn on the cob on a winter's evening, reading
stories to each other, or putting on small plays. The six
siblings cared for and looked out for one another, even as
adults. There is however, one formal family photo that shows
the young adults sitting with their parents, dressed in their
best, all looking in different directions, obviously miffed
about something. John and Mattie look especially peeved, and
this picture always makes me laugh, indicating as it does that
things were not always harmonious.

There are other words to describe Grace's life;
disappointment, sorrow, self-denial, regret, loss, lack. A good
deal of the drama came from her in-laws, who thought my
grandfather, Grover, married "beneath" him. The young
couple lived with his parents for the first six years of their

marriage, and this gave many opportunities for Grace to be controlled and treated with condescension. When Grover took a job as a railroad mechanic, they moved from Decatur to Roodhouse with their two young daughters, giving Grace a bit of freedom from what had been some intense female oppression. She continued to hold her tongue at family gatherings to keep the peace, but in 1929, the year she was pregnant with my mother, her fifth and last child, she finally had enough. A 39-year-old woman, she spoke up for herself, letting it be known she would no longer be silent and abused.

Her mother-in-law Fannie chastised and belittled her on a regular basis, and began her regular rant on a visit to Roodhouse. "You should have never let this happen! How can you think about having another baby! You are putting such a burden on everyone...how will you be able to afford another baby?" she said. Apparently Grace stood up out of her chair, poked her finger in Fannie's tiny, pinched face and told her not to speak another word if she ever expected to come back to the house and see her grandchildren ever again. "You're going to sit there and you are going to listen to me, and you're not going to say a word till I finish," she said.

That day she unleashed the more than 10 years of grievances she'd borne since joining the family, and never allowed herself to be derided by Fannie, or Grover's sister Flora, again.

There were times when Grace felt she missed her chance at a better life because of her broken romance with Charles Drake, a young doctor. Smart, slim and ambitious, he took her to concerts and art exhibits. However, as time passed there was no offer of marriage, and when he moved to Chicago the relationship ended.

By the time he realized he wanted to marry her, Grace was days away from marrying Grover. Drake sent a letter stating he hoped he wasn't too late, as he'd heard she was to marry and he wanted her to reconsider. Though she had waited for this man, and apparently loved him, she did not reply. I imagine her standing for a moment after reading it (she actually kept his letter under the dresser scarf in her bedroom for years), thinking of how to stop what she'd put into motion and go to Chicago. My mother says Grandma told her, "I just couldn't hurt your grandfather like that," and so she married my grandpa, a horse trainer, electrician and rounder.

This story is so intriguing to me because she was a high school graduate, which in the early 1900s was the top achievement for most girls, and though she was a product of a working class family, she had an interest in the world, in travel, in books and music and art. Drake was more suitable for who she was inside, a person who was interested in ideas, in the world outside of Decatur. He saw her worth, though acted on it too late. She aspired to be more than she was, and had to push against her family in order to become more of herself. Her parents were hoping to convince their shy, non-assertive daughter to stay single, live at home and care for them in their old age. I can remember being horrified by this story, unable to sympathize with people who would so thoroughly determine the outcome of another human being's life.

So, after graduation she took a job as a telephone operator, and one day, long after Mr. Drake had made his exit, a crew of electricians came in to work on the wiring. One friendly member of the group kept borrowing paper from her. She finally realized he was flirting. While the men came back the next several days to finish their work, she cautiously flirted back (Charles Drake be damned!) and Grandpa eventually won the approval of the redheaded beauty.

The life I imagine she would have had with a Chicago doctor is a definite contrast with the one she had with my grandpa. When he took the job in Roodhouse, it did allow the family to get away from his parents, jealous sister and pestering sister-in-law, but it came at the price of small town life. Roodhouse with its 2,700 population could not offer the opportunities of Decatur, a small city of 30,000. Though he always had a job and was an involved father and faithful husband, Grandpa was more of a cowboy, smoking his pipe in the evening reading Zane Grey stories, quite the opposite to what I imagine to be the more urbane Drake. My mother used to quote Grandma who apparently said, "Whenever I doubt what I've done with my life, all I have to do is look at you children." She did have doubts, as so many people do. Most relationships are not pure, grand loves, but are built on the need to survive in this world, to have something; a child, a friend, a home. She wished for something different, at times, but ultimately found her way, as many women do, through connection with friends and children, and the humble love of a good, hard-working man.

Missing Mimi
By Aline Weiller

Holding my eldest cousin in her arms, my Columbian grandmother cooed, "Tu eres mia." Spanish for "You are mine." As babies sometimes do, little Lorraine mimicked what she'd heard, but with a twist nicknaming my grandmother "Mimia." It stuck. My immediate family shortened it to Mimi.

Our matriarch, Mimi was a strong, beautiful South American, but blonde with a fair complexion framing light brown eyes. She had a thin nose and lips, with fine hair pulled back in her signature, soft bun. She was seldom, if ever, seen with loose locks.

She and my grandfather, Carlos, whom we called Papa, had seven children and relocated to New York from Bogota in the 1930s. Amidst her joys, Mimi endured great sorrow. Her first daughter died at one, her fourth son, at thirty-three. She was also widowed for over two decades. Mimi always lived nearby and was a positive force in my childhood. My two sisters, brother and I were her play dates at the ready.

We ate well at Mimi's, always welcomed with fresh sopa de papa, potato soup before almost every meal. The consummate babysitter, Mimi reinforced manners, reminding us what fork to use and to place napkins on our laps. She lived with her children's nanny turned housekeeper, named Julita, and a series of loving dogs. Mimi and Julita were a good team. Both enjoyed cooking and church; they reveled in authentic Colombian fare and watching Sunday Catholic mass on television, when they couldn't attend. Julita often taught us to pray, guiding our small hands in the sign of the cross, until we got it right, clasping them at the gesture's end.

"En el nombre del Padre, y del Hijo y del Espíritu Santo...Amen," she'd say. Mimi would give a slight nod and smile, approving of our religion tutorial.

Though more feminine in her golden years, Mimi was a star basketball player and tomboyish prankster in her youth. Family folklore has kept her antics alive, among them the time she covered stones with gravy and placed them on Papa's dish as part of the evening meal, nearly ending their courtship. Cut from a more formal cloth, my grandfather did not find it funny, though I've always enjoyed a hushed chuckle at the tale's recounting.

Mimi, too, was an artist—a painter skilled with both a brush and at crafts. An early Martha Stewart, she fashioned my birthday hats and blowers from pink crepe paper, my color of choice. She was always up for a party. Holidays were lavish with traditional Spanish food and lively chatter, her house packed with at least two generations. Christmas was especially memorable as Mimi built a pesebre or nativity scene of mammoth proportions. She painted a large sky backdrop and mountains, then layered two tables with hundreds of clay figurines. She even made the local newspaper for her creative effort.

In her early 80s, Mimi began losing her sight and the pesebre became a challenge. I offered to help set it up. With her pinpoint vision and my teenage sense for the aesthetic, together we'd recreate the creche. She knew each figure by heart, but palmed their faces for reassurance.

"Aline, hand me Los Reyes Magos," Mimi would say. I'd search and unwrap the ancient Three Kings set.

"These Mimi?" I'd asked.

"Yes, mijita," Mimi confirmed, clutching each figure tightly. I guided her hands toward the Kings' proper placement, en route to the manger.

Both shepherds and saints graced the pesebre, with barn animals scattered about. It was her masterpiece. Mimi had a special fondness for Santa Lucia—Saint Lucy—her namesake and also, the patron Saint of Sight. She always perked up when I unearthed that statue.

My mother now has the pesebre collection and continues Mimi's December tradition. Last Christmas she parted with a few pieces, giving them to me as presents. They stirred scenes from my childhood and days as Mimi's apprentice.

Joyful, Mimi always sang as we built the nativity scene from scratch. I had a private art and life lesson each Advent, as she taught me how to balance the pesebre figures by size and color. She also urged me to embrace fun, nudging me to play a joke or two on my siblings, like temporarily hiding their toys. Mimi grasped life's upside despite her losses and told me to expect great things. To Mimi, life was for the taking. She instilled in me a spirited sense of adventure, encouraging travel and the pursuit of my writing. She taught me to pay my respects, in the form of food or a sympathy card. And to take risks, like living in Manhattan and starting a career, a pale comparison to the brave move from her homeland to America. Mimi taught me Spanish and to take pride in our heritage. She conveyed the importance of forgiveness and never letting others rob me of my joy. Her wisdom still carries me in my roles as daughter, sister, wife and parent.

When Mimi developed dementia, she became more homebound. I'd grocery shop for her and stay for dinner, listening to tales of Colombia and beyond. Always wanting to remain at home, Mimi was granted her wish as we provided live-in help during her final years. She kept her witty candor, even with her ailing health. And never lost her spunk, still relishing a laugh with the grandchildren.

"Buy me a lottery ticket, Aline," Mimi would say. Each week I'd oblige; it kept her going.

Though Mimi's sight and energy waned, she asked my mother to take her to church just weeks before she died. I accompanied them. The visiting priest didn't know Mimi, but we asked him to pray over her. He paraphrased Scripture, his spotted hand upon her brow.

"Kings and prophets have longed to see as you have seen, but have not. You see with the eyes of faith," the priest said. He was on target—Mimi saw with her heart. She was pure love.

Some say people choose their moment of death. Mimi died with her nurse at her side, while the extended family was at a grandchild's wedding; she wouldn't have wanted to disrupt our celebration. Though my loss is marked by a palpable void, Mimi's was an unassuming goodbye that garnered a peaceful respect.

Nessie

By Victoria Horsham

It was well past midnight and I was still sorting my belongings into boxes. Leaving an old home for a new one is always a mixture of excitement and terror, but leaving for the first time is hardest. It's especially difficult when you're a teenager with too strong an attachment to your mountains of stuff, trying to decide what things are important enough to deserve precious space in the tiny dorm room you'll soon be living in, and what you'll be leaving in a box outside the nearest charity shop.

The ceramic pig collection my aunt had given me went in the donations pile, as did most of the small collection of stuffed toys that I still felt a little guilty for getting rid of. Out went my old school books and most of my collection of rocks and shells—all the pretty ones, at least. The ones with genuine value for my studies were already nestled safe in their own little box, wrapped carefully with newspaper and tape, lest any of the minute details get lost from them scraping against one another.

My mum was feeling the stress and grief of it all as well, possibly worse than I was, and it wasn't long before she started shouting at me to hurry up, wanting to get the pain of saying goodbye to her only daughter over more quickly, like ripping off a plaster. I complied, and hurried up. Dragging a donations box over to a shelf, I ran an arm along it, spilling the dusty keepsakes into it and on the floor. I knelt to pick up the lost knick-knacks, tossing them in haphazardly.

Then I noticed the little flash of turquoise peeking out from under the dust and fly carcasses. A few seconds of panicked rummaging and I had all the pieces; one head, a tail and three humps, making up a little ceramic Loch Ness Monster that, placed on a shelf, almost looked nothing like it was swimming along. It was a silly, slightly ugly little thing, the turquoise paint applied with a childish hand and the eyes wild, painted so it looked as though the creature was cross-eyed. It was my great-grandmother's.

I don't have many solid memories of Grandma Jess. I can't remember her voice, or how she laughed, or how she smelled. She was quiet, unassuming and generally took a back seat in my world to her big bear of a husband, and their playful bachelor son with the endless hilarious anecdotes. But what she was, more than anything else, was there. Quietly bustling around behind the scenes and gently listening to me twitter on like small children do. During my visits I'd spend the evenings curled up on the floor in front of the TV, playing with the brass figurines they kept on the shelf, or with Grandma Jess' button tin, while Grandma knitted and Grandpa napped and my great-uncle watched the news.

Shortly after I learned to read, I was allowed to look at some of the books that covered the big wall behind Grandma Jess' knitting chair. I almost immediately became obsessed with the one book I found that had pictures, a mythology book I think, although it didn't have any stories in—and it was far from the sort of book most adults would offer to a child. It was a book of monsters and strange beasts, but there were no sweet stories of friendly fairies or playful pixies, just page after page of strange, old-world black and white pictures of monsters, with a few paragraphs describing each one and what it did. There were mermaids with bare breasts and mouths full of shark teeth, massive black dogs with glowing eyes, and hollow-eyed, lanky creatures that knelt in dark pools, and foreign monsters that looked like tigers with human faces and women's breasts.

Many adults would have balked at letting a small child look at a book like that, but Grandma Jess just sat me on her lap, opened the fragile pages and helped me with the long words, listening to me fumble them with infinite patience and hugging me closer when I successfully mouthed my way around something complicated. I was fascinated by that book, and although I couldn't manage all the longer words, it became the only book I would read before bed. It became our regular thing, something we got to do together, just the two of us, when Grandpa was napping and my great-uncle was busy with the TV.

One evening, as Grandma Jess brought me in a mug of hot milk to settle me to sleep, she placed a little box down in front of me.

Inside was the Nessie figurine. To my child's eyes it was beautiful—brightly colored, and completely different from anything I'd seen before. The thick ceramic was sturdy enough to be safe for a clumsy child like me to play with, and I was half convinced it was a piece of rare treasure. It was Grandma Jess'; one of the many little delights her house held. But this was better than the little wooden clocks I helped her wind by pulling on the thick iron weights, or the giant soup mugs with their retro designs and recipes printed on the front. It was even better than the wall of ancient books, which smelled enticingly of old paper and had exciting sounding titles on the sides, but were mostly too difficult for me to read. Because this was something I recognized from the book, albeit more colorful and less monstrous-looking than the Nessie my mythology book had described. And even better, I then learned, it was mine.

The Nessie had spent the last few decades on Grandma Jess' vanity in her bedroom, where I never went, but now she'd decided it was time little Nessie had a new home, and since I loved monsters almost as much as she did, the figurine could stay with me.

I wanted to know what she meant, about loving monsters as much as I did. But Grandma Jess wasn't around for much longer, after that. A stroke sent her to a nursing home, and when I went to visit she just sat in a chair and stared out into the space a few inches past my head, never blinked, never said a word. My family didn't take me to visit her again, and she died a few weeks later. I was too young to really understand it all, but I knew that thinking about my Grandma made me feel sad—too sad to talk about her to anyone. So the years passed by, and I didn't ask anyone about the monsters she loved, and eventually I forgot. And the little Nessie figurine sat on my bookshelf in my room, gathering dust.

My mum called up to me again from downstairs, waking me out of my daydream. I carefully cleaned the figurine, wrapped each piece in newspaper, and placed the pieces in the box with my important rocks for study, where I knew they'd be safe, then dusted myself off, and went downstairs, to ask my mum why Grandma loved monsters.

CONTRIBUTORS

Roy A. Barnes writes from the plains of southeastern Wyoming. His poetry and prose have been featured at a number of magazines and websites.

Gabriella Brand's fiction, essays, and poetry have appeared in *Room Magazine, StepAway, The Binnacle, The First Line, The Christian Science Monitor,* and several anthologies. One of her short stories was nominated for a Pushcart Prize in 2014. Gabriella divides her time between New England, where she teaches languages, and Quebec, where she canoes, hikes, and writes. She travels widely, mostly on foot.

Julie Brown teaches adult special education at a local community college. She spends her free time reading, playing with her grandchildren, riding her bike, and now writing essays and short stories. This is her first publication.

Melanie Bryant holds an MFA in Creative Writing from the University of New Orleans. She currently works as a professional freelance food writer for a number of online and print magazines. When not stirring up her latest creations in the kitchen, Melanie is working on her craft.

Originally from Seattle, WA, **Kim Bussing** is currently an English major at Georgetown University and has studied creative writing at Cambridge University. Her fiction has appeared in a variety of other publications. When not writing, she's working her way through a lengthy to-read list, running in the rain, and drinking too much coffee. You can find her on Twitter or browsing a used bookstore.

Cherise Charleswell wears many Womanist hats: Clinical Researcher/Diversity Officer for the Huntington Medical Research Institutes, Women's Issues Chair at The Hampton Institute, Chair of the National Women's Studies Association

Social Justice Task Force, President of the Southern California Public Health Association and CEO of the website Eclectic Life.

Dawn Corrigan has published poetry and prose in a number of print and online journals and anthologies. Her debut novel, an environmental mystery called *Mitigating Circumstances*, was published by Five Star/Cengage in January 2014. Currently she's working on a family saga set in Hell's Kitchen. She lives in Gulf Breeze, Florida.

Terri Elders recently returned to Southern California, where she continues to write about her life's adventures. She blogs at **atouchoftarragon.blogspot.com**

Joan Gary is a British born Jamaican living abroad. Writing about memories has become her welcome pastime.

Jamie Grabert earned a Bachelor of Arts degree in English, with Emphasis in Creative Writing. She has been a full-time freelance writer for 13 years, and in her spare time, helps care for her grandmother, who often sits with Jamie while she's writing and offers on the spot critiques.

Krysten Lindsay Hager is the author of the *Landry's True Colors Series*, a clean reads young adult series. Krysten writes about self-esteem, fitting in, and friendship in *True Colors* and *Best Friends...Forever?*

Savannah Hendricks is the author of *Nonnie and I,* a story about the friendship between a giraffe and a little girl set in Botswana. She is also co-author of *Child Genius 101: The Ultimate Guide to Early Childhood Development (Vol 1, 2 & 3).* You can learn more by visiting her blog **The Sea Shells of Life**.

Victoria Horsham was born in the early 80s in Essex, England. An unrepentant nerd, she grew up devouring sci-fi, fantasy and horror novels as fast as her local library could supply them. With a small number of short published works under her belt, she's currently working on a collection of stories that she hopes to see published in the future.

Lynn Jarrett is a freelance writer with an Associate's of Applied Science degree from Oklahoma State University. She enjoys reading, writing, and keeping in touch with friends and relatives. She previously worked in the legal field, retired from state government, and served as a volunteer firefighter/emergency medical technician for 19 years. She lives in rural central Oklahoma and currently works at the public library.

Kristina Jensen is a 'poet afloat', freelance writer and musician, living a life of voluntary simplicity in the Marlborough Sounds of New Zealand. She is an enthusiastic advocate of spending as much time in nature as possible and enjoys wild food foraging, sailing and collecting weird bits of driftwood. Her poetry has been published in *Eclecticism*, *REM*, *Shotglass*, *The Shine Journal*, *Valley Micropress*, *Takahe*, *Cyclamens & Swords*, and other publications.

Rhi Myfanwy Kirkland attended the University of Calgary. She graduated with a degree in political science and religious studies. She currently lives in Calgary, Alberta, Canada working as a freelance journalist and photographer.

Chynna Laird is a mother of four, a freelance writer and an award-winning author. Her passion is helping children and families living with Sensory Processing Disorder (SPD) and other special needs. She's authored two children's book, two memoirs, a Young Adult novella, a Young Adult paranormal/suspense series (The Watcher series), a New Adult contemporary novel and an adult suspense/thriller. Website: **www.chynnalairdauthor.ca**

A criminal court reporter by day, **Jody Lebel** mainly writes romantic suspense novels but her short stories have sold to *Woman's World* magazine, *Chicken Soup for the Soul*, *Cosmo UK*, and dozens of others. Her book, titled *Playing Dead*, was released by The Wild Rose Press to excellent reviews. Jody was raised in charming New England, was an only child who had an only child (claiming she didn't breed well in captivity) and now lives with her two cats in southern Florida.

MK McFadden is the writer of short stories, screenplays, and opinion articles. She spends most of her time reading, watching TV and trying new recipes. She currently lives in South Carolina.

Gargi Mehra writes fiction and essays that have appeared in numerous literary magazines. She blogs at **gargimehra.wordpress.com** and tweets as **@gargimehra.**

Marilyn Morgan is a retired English teacher. She lives and writes in Central New York State. Marilyn's prose has been published in *Edge, Motif, Five Quarterly* and others. Her poetry has appeared in *Atlas Poetica, Bright Stars, Red Lights, A Hundred Gourds, American Tanka* and others.

William Poe is the author of *African-Americans of Calvert County*. For over a decade he has collected oral histories and photographs of Calvert County's black community. His poems, essays, and photographs have been published in several magazines and literary journals.

Vanessa Raney is an American living in Croatia and studying the Croatian language. Her first bilingual chapbook, The *Idea of Woman,* is forthcoming from Dancing Girl Press in late 2015.

Gerard Sarnat received his education at Harvard and Stanford. He established and staffed clinics for the disenfranchised, has been a CEO of healthcare organizations, and was a Stanford professor. Gerry is the author of three critically acclaimed collections: *Homeless Chronicles from Abraham to Burning Man* (2010), *Disputes* (2012), *and 17s* (2014). For Huffington Post reviews, reading dates including Stanford, publications and more, visit **GerardSarnat.com.** His books are available at select bookstores and on Amazon. Gerard has been featured this year as Songs of

Eretz Poetry Review's Poet of the Week, with one of his poems appearing daily. Dr. Sarnat is the second poet ever to be so honored.

Terri Scott realized that her grandmother's sharp wit and sense of humor was genetic. However, it would take another 30 years for Terri to produce creative non-fiction—she's writing her memoir, *The Filly From Philly*. She can be reached **@Positive_Twist**

Multiple award-winning author, **Jacqueline Seewald**, has taught creative, expository and technical writing at Rutgers University as well as high school English. She also worked as both an academic librarian and an educational media specialist. Fifteen of her books of fiction have been published to critical praise. Her short stories, poems, essays, reviews and articles have appeared in hundreds of diverse publications and numerous anthologies such as *The Writer, L.A. Times, Pedestal, Sherlock Holmes Mystery Magazine, Library Journal, and Publishers Weekly.*

Robyn Segal is a freelance writer and has been published in several publications including *Dr. TJ Eckelburg Review, Workzine, Literary Yard, and Gravel Magazine.* She lives in Massachusetts with her wife and four children.

Lesley Sheridan is a freelance writer from Maysville, Kentucky, who lives for Pinterest boards, animal print high heels and combinable coupon codes. An agreeable loner, she's high maintenance but assumes she's low maintenance, and she wholeheartedly prefers the company of cats to people. She dedicates this narrative to her feisty grandmother, Kathryn Johnson, and her supportive father, Herbie Johnson, who is and will always be her hero.

Pat St. Pierre has been writing poetry, fiction, and nonfiction since her high school days. She tries to capture small vignettes of life and writes about them. She writes for both adults and children. Her third poetry book, *Full Circle*, was recently published by Kelsay Books and is available at **Amazon.com**.

Her poems and fiction have been widely published. You may find some of her work at: *A Long Story Short, Fiction 365, The Camel Saloon, The Feathered Flounder, Daily Love, Kids Imagination Train, Proquest,* etc. She also has a love of photography and her work has been recognized both online and in print. Many of her photos have been on covers. You may find her photos at: *Mountain Tales Press, Decades Review, Ken*Again, Front Porch Review, Gravel,* etc. Her blog is **www.pstpierre.wordpress.com.**

Stephanie Rose is a marine biologist and freelance writer. She has recently completed a Masters in Aquatic Pathobiology and has written two research papers to be released in the next year. Writing remains one of her greatest passions.

Safiullah Rafai is a 12-year-old seventh grader from the Washington DC metro area. He enjoys basketball and is an active student who is passionate about community service. He started writing at the age of 7 when he wrote a letter and received a response from President Obama. Safiullah lives with his parents, one older, and one younger brother.

Wendy Tanzer was born in Vancouver, BC Canada. Her grandmother was "terribly British"—though Welsh, by birth—and the story above is just one of the many secrets she shared. Another is the "proper" way to make a damn fine pot of tea!

Cathy Thomason is a retired librarian. When not writing, she travels, reads, hikes and does volunteer work. Cats are her pet of choice. She lives with her husband in Port Hueneme, California.

Chelsea Uchytil and her brother Chad are twins for the record books. In 1991 their grandmother Arlette Schweitzer was a surrogate mother for her own daughter and the first person in America to give birth to her own grandchildren. Chelsea currently works as a primary caregiver at the family-owned assisted living home in Rapid City, South Dakota.

R.C. Van Horn, a graduate of Bowdoin College, lives and writes in Boston, Massachusetts. She loves words and dogs, in no particular order, and dreams of moving back to Vermont.

Karen Warinsky G. Karen Warinsky was a finalist in the 2013 Montreal International Poetry Contest and a semi-finalist in 2011. The top 50 poems were published in an anthology printed by Véhicule Press.

Aline Weiller is a journalist, essayist and guest blogger whose work has been published in Brain, Child: The Magazine for Thinking Mothers, Mamalode, Role Reboot, Your Teen, Skirt, Scary Mommy, Erma Bombeck Writers' Workshop and Grown and Flown, among others. She's also the CEO/Founder of the public relations firm, Wordsmith, LLC, based in Connecticut, where she lives with her husband and two sons.

Mariana Williams is the author of *Love, Regret and Accidental Nudity*: a collection of OMG moments sorted into six categories. It was a finalist in the Humor Category of the 2014 International Book Awards. Prior to this memoir, Mariana penned the Veronica Bennett Series of romance, comedy, and accidental crime: *Happy New Year, Darling, The Valentine State*—a finalist in the 2014 Chick Lit category of International Book Award, and Stars or Stripes 4th of July, which won a 2011 Indie Excellence Book Award. She produces Long Beach Searches for Greatest Storyteller, a city-wide competition in Long Beach, California, now in its fifth year.

Suzan L. Wiener has had numerous poems, articles, personal experience stories, and other shorter pieces published in major publications such as *Mature Living, Mature Years, Mocha Memoirs, Verses, Reader's Digest, The Saturday Evening Post, FellowScript, The Writer's Ezine*, etc. She also has two e-books published, entitled *Quiet, Please* and *Happy Halloween!*, of which she is most proud.

ABOUT THE AUTHOR

Editor **Robyn McGee** is an author, college professor and a popular guest speaker who shares stories of love, loss and enduring power of family. Robyn has written two other nonfiction books, *Hungry For More: A Keeping it Real Guide for Black Women on Weight and Body Image* and the sci-fi themed *California Nightmares*. Robyn's own Grandmother story "Estelle Out of Bounds" is headed for the Los Angeles theater.

Tweet Robyn @ladieswhohowl

A special thanks to the 40 remarkable writers who contributed to this book. Your stories shared will inspire and amaze many.

To Tee for your love and support through your own loss. You mean the world to me.

To Paul thanks for your honesty, wordsmith ways and decades of friendship.

To Grandmaster Jerome A. Harris, Sr. Many thanks for all the laughter and life lessons. You bring out the warrior in me.

To all the Grandmothers of the world, past, present and future.

Author's info:

Robyn McGee is the author of *Hungry For More: A Keeping it Real Guide For Black Women on Weight and Body Image*, (Seal Press 2006), *California Nightmares*, a book about futuristic author Octavia Butler, and numerous articles and blogs. Follow Robyn on Twitter **@LadiesWhoHowl** and her website **www.writerswhorock.com**.

order at pegasusbooks.net

CPSIA information can be obtained at www.ICGtesting.com
Printed in the USA
LVOW07s0021290615

444203LV00004B/88/P